With Their Whole Strength

WITH THEIR WHOLE STRENGTH

WILLIAM
WILSON

NAZARETH BOOKS
Doubleday & Company, Inc.
Garden City, New York
1981

ISBN: 0-385-17435-7
Library of Congress Catalog Card Number: 80-2084
Copyright © 1981 by The Catholic Heritage Press, Inc.
Printed in the United States of America
First Edition

For Anne
a patient wife
and a superb critic

Other titles in series:

Contents

Contents

1.

Who Is a Hero?

One aim of this book is to explode a myth: You don't have to be John Wayne to be a hero. One kind of heroism does show itself in physical courage. Firemen need it to save people from burning buildings. Thousands of soldiers needed it to free Europe and the world from the threat of Nazi tyranny and end the holocaust that sought to stamp out the Jewish people. We'd be lost without it. But, "Damn the torpedoes, full speed ahead," isn't the only way to give voice to courage.

Bravery is a big part of being a hero. It takes courage to stand quietly while a riot squad is getting ready to turn a fire hose on you. It takes courage to work with people who have a horribly ugly disease, knowing that you may catch the disease from them. But bravery doesn't mean that a hero never feels fear. What sets a hero apart is that he or she acts in spite of the fear.

Some heroes are famous. Lord Nelson, parading the quarterdeck of H.M.S. *Victory* in full-dress uniform at the battle of Trafalgar, was such a hero. His officers warned him that his uniform made him a ready target for enemy snipers. His reply was that it also made him obvious to his men, who needed all the encouragement they could find. Nelson died, and he was enshrined as one of the greatest heroes of the British people. Ballads were composed in his honor, and a huge monument was erected in his honor in Trafalgar Square. But many heroes never win public applause. Parents spend years caring for a retarded child, wearing themselves out and spending whatever money they have to keep the child alive. They do what they do, not because anyone holds a gun to their head or stages a parade in their honor, but because of love and respect for the life God has committed to their care.

One big act can make a hero. Sam Houston and Davy Crockett died at the Alamo, and the United States will never forget them. Some people's heroism is made up of many small acts. A mother in Harlem scrubs floors at night so that her son can go to medical school. What she does is every bit as courageous as Crockett's willingness to face the onslaught of Santa Ana's army.

The hero comes in many shapes and colors, in both sexes, and at all stages of life. By breaking new ground when others fear to do so, or by defending important parts of what we have inherited from the past, the hero lets us know that some things are more valuable than comfort and pleasure. He shows us that some things are worth taking an unpopular stand for, going to jail for, dying for.

People become heroes for different reasons. Not all heroes believe in God, much less the God of Abraham. Heroes are atheists, Buddhists, Muslims. Some are good people, people of deep faith and compassion, whose belief, whatever it may be, is the driving force behind their heroism. Some heroes are not very nice people, but when a moment of crisis hits, something in them is touched, and it catapults them to greatness.

This book takes a look at ten heroes, all men, all believers, whose heroic acts were powered by their faith. The second aim of the book is to show that faith is for heroes, not for sissies. The men in this book were strong individuals who endured great suffering in order to achieve great things. None was physically violent. All were humble. But they definitely were not sissies.

Occasionally, I have had to imagine or modernize the conversations in these stories, and in doing so, I have tried to be faithful to the spirit of the individual whose life is being told. In the spirit of these men, the reader may find a spark of greatness for his own life. If "it is better to light one candle than to curse the darkness," then one candle can also light another.

—William J. Wilson
Alexandria, Virginia

1.
Charles
de Foucauld

Hermit

Charles Eugene Viscount de Foucauld was a man of extremes. As a cadet at France's elite Saint Cyr Military Academy, he competed fiercely for scholastic honors, yet within one year of finishing a distinguished academic career, he was drummed out of the French army. It is not easy to be thrown out of a military organization on charges of improper morals. Military service has more often been a refuge for young men whose conduct has gotten them into trouble. A barracks is not a monastery; and military superiors ordinarily tolerate such things as drunkenness or gambling as an understandable, if regrettable, way of dealing with the pressures of life in uniform. Yet in the rough-and-tumble of the French occupation of Algeria a century ago, Charles de Foucauld became a disgrace to the uniform he wore. He was stripped of his rank and expelled from the military for "indiscipline and notorious misconduct."

However, as soon as the young nobleman was thrown out of the army, he sought to get back in. Foucauld learned that his regiment was about to march against a rebel force at Bou Hamama and, whatever his vices, cowardice was not among them. He asked to be restored to rank for the duration of the campaign so that he might fight alongside his comrades and, if need be, die with them. His request was granted, he soldiered bravely until the rebels were defeated, and then he resigned his commission. But he did not leave North Africa. He volunteered to explore Morocco as an undercover intelligence agent for the French government, and for two years he traveled in disguise, speaking Arabic, living as a native, sharing the food of the desert nomads. His mission was to explore the Moroccan countryside, learn the habits of the people, scout areas where good fortifications might be built, and discover where hostile tribesmen gathered and how strong they were as potential enemies.

The work was dangerous. One slip in Arabic while squatting around the caravan fire for the evening meal, and the Frenchman's blood would quickly stain the desert sand. After two years of living on the knife's edge, Charles de Foucauld emerged from the trackless desert, mission completed, and published his widely acclaimed *Reconnaissance au Maroc*, a masterpiece in shrewd observation, painstaking data gathering, and brilliant analysis.

At twenty-six Foucauld had chalked up an accomplishment that many men would be happy to have as the final triumph of a life's work. Yet he emerged from the desert sunk in despair, gripped by doubt, and beginning to think that some sort of belief might hold the clue to lessening his misery. He would later tell a friend that he knew the source of his unhappiness: "For twelve years I lived without any faith," he would recall; "I was twelve years believing and denying nothing, despairing of the truth, and not even believing in God."

By the time he emerged from the sun-blistered Sahara, however, cracks had begun to appear in the stone wall of Charles de Foucauld's unbelief. Caravan routes and potential fortifications were not the only things to come under the Frenchman's watchful gaze as he roamed the desert. His wanderings had brought him in close contact with both Muslims and Jews. In them, he saw people whose religion was not confined to parroting catechism questions or fearing to incur the wrath of God by missing church. He saw their devotion to the rituals of their religion and heard them discuss their beliefs and rules of conduct. More importantly, he came to see that Islam and Judaism touched every corner of a person's life, giving that life a meaning and a goal. "Islam shook me deeply," he said later. "Seeing such faith, seeing people living in the continual presence of God, I came to glimpse something bigger and more real than worldly occupations."

For a while, it seemed the ex-soldier's brilliant mind might stand in the way of his ever finding a God to whom he could commit himself. Throughout his adolescence and adulthood, Foucauld had made his mark by his wits. First, at Saint Cyr and, later, during his desert exploration, he had poked and probed at reality with his intellect, slicing up problems with his rapierlike mind until they yielded solutions to his relentless assault.

After returning to France and settling near his

kinfolk in Paris, he went at faith the same way. Consumed by a desire to wrestle an answer from life about its meaning and its source, the same young man who had been thrown out of the army for living a foul life began to live like a monk, spending long hours reading the great works of Greek philosophy to see if he might find the key to his restlessness. He found a love of virtue, but at the level at which his troubled soul hungered and thirsted, he found "nothing but emptiness and disgust."

One day he happened to pick up a book given him by a cousin years earlier, a collection of sermons by the French bishop, Bossuet. He devoured the theologian's beautiful language and the more beautiful picture he sketched of what the Christian might become. As Foucauld's search intensified, his prayer became, "My God, if you exist, help me to know you!"

As so often happens the moment a soul expresses a willingness to change, God responded with a generosity that was overwhelming. Foucauld's heart, as well as his eyes, were opened. He grew close again to the only family he had left—his aunt, Madame Moitessier, and his cousin, Marie, Madame de Bondy. He saw in the lives led by these good women—lives he had once laughed at—a beauty and a source of inspiration that now encouraged his own search for God.

Still looking to approach God through his mind, Foucauld continued to pray "Help me to know you" until a chance meeting at his aunt's house changed his life. He had decided to seek out a learned priest who would tutor him in the Christian religion. He wanted to study dutifully, learn all he could, and then, having completed his examination as if he were taking a course of studies, decide whether Christianity was worth believing.

Such, however, was not to be the case. Madame Moitessier had a close friend, Abbé Huvelin, who was both holy and learned. When Foucauld approached him to become the instructor for his self-prescribed crash course in religion, Father Huvelin, with the shrewdness born of prayerful contact with God and long hours spent counseling souls, refused to take the bait. Charles asked to be instructed. The priest told him, instead, to kneel down and make a confession. Then, he told him to take Communion immediately. There are times in life when action, not thought or words, is needed, and to his credit, Father Huvelin saw that Charles de Foucauld was at precisely such a point. To his credit, the young French nobleman did as he was told. Thus began a lifelong relationship of spiritual counselor and student that was to end only with Father Huvelin's death. Foucauld submitted to his guide for every major decision. He would sometimes let his teacher know the answer he hoped to receive, but he would not go back on his commitment to submit himself to the priest's judgment. Seventeen years after their first meeting, feeling an intense urge to remove himself further from civilization and trek deeper into the Sahara, he wrote the abbé for advice. "Write or telegraph and I shall obey you," he told his spiritual guide. "My own feeling is quite definitely that I should leave on 10 January."

If he had traveled a roundabout route to find

God, Charles de Foucauld did not lose much time plunging into God's service. At Christmastime in 1888, he arrived in the Holy Land, a pilgrim to the places where Jesus had walked—Bethlehem, Jerusalem, Nazareth. Nazareth especially fascinated him. Gradually, he came to feel that he wanted to walk in those footsteps, seeking to relive in his own life the poverty, obscurity, and humility that had marked Jesus' life at Nazareth.

In a sense, the remainder of Foucauld's life was a postscript to that first pilgrimage, for he would spend the next twenty-seven years trying to live out the insights into the life of Jesus that had come to him as he walked the streets of the town where Jesus had lived. The key to all that Charles de Foucauld would later achieve can be found in the lessons of humility and service he learned at Nazareth. "I do not think," he would one day write, "there is a Gospel phrase that has made a deeper impression on me and transformed my life more than this one: 'Insofar as you did this to one of the least of these brothers of mine, you did it to me."

The next stop on Foucauld's pilgrimage of the spirit was at the French Trappist monastery of Our Lady of the Snows. The Cistercians gave him the name Brother Marie-Alberic, and during the six months he spent there as a novice, they taught him the spirituality of Saint Benedict and trained him in the particularly rigid form of the Benedictine rule followed by the Trappists. Even that iron regime was not enough, and the new religious asked to be sent to the poorest monastery the Trappists had. His request was granted. In June 1890, he was transferred to the monastery of Our Lady of the Sacred Heart at Akbes in Syria. For seven years Foucauld remained lost in this spot in an obscure corner of Asia Minor, yet even the most ramshackled and impoverished community of an order dedicated to poverty and obscurity could not fully satisfy the thirst of Brother Marie-Alberic for the "little life of Nazareth" that Jesus led. He wrote to the father general of the Cistercian order and expressed a desire to leave the community, not to return to the world but to live as a hermit.

Only after the chief abbot of the Trappists agreed that he did, indeed, seem to have a calling to the solitary life, did Foucauld take the name Brother Charles of Jesus and leave the community at Akbes. He journeyed to Nazareth and plunged into obscurity, as he had once plunged into vice. He became the gardener and handyman for the Poor Clare's convent in Nazareth, and in return for his work, the sisters gave him such scanty meals as he ate and a rough wooden lean-to for his house. Resting clumsily against one wall of the convent, the dilapidated little shack had been a tool shed until Brother Charles claimed it for his hermit's cell.

He was as happy as a child at Christmas. "This is the very life I have been looking for," he said, describing in glowing terms the opportunity his new life gave him to practice poverty, solitude, self-effacement, humble work, and most important of all, "complete obscurity, the most perfect possible imitation of the life of our Lord Jesus as he must have lived it in Nazareth." For three years, Brother Charles of Jesus lived more happily than he had ever lived before, finding his God by losing himself. It was as if he were trying to prove in his own daily existence the words of Jesus: "Unless a grain of wheat falls on the ground and dies, it remains just one grain. But if it dies, it yields a great harvest."

If complete obscurity was one foundation stone of Brother Charles's inner life, the presence of Jesus in the Eucharist was another. His was not the faith of a theologian, making neat distinctions about how, when, and why Jesus chose to leave the memorial of his Body and Blood under the appearance of bread and wine. For him, where the communion wafer was present, Jesus was present, just as totally and truly as he had been in Nazareth as a human being two thousand years ago. In the mind-boggling obscurity of a piece of bread, the love of Jesus had found a way to stay behind with those who would follow in his name and in his footsteps. As long as he had that contact, Brother Charles lacked nothing.

Yet this contact, so central to his own search for God, led Brother Charles to realize that he could not stay in Nazareth, could not continue in the kind of humble service that had filled his life for three years. He felt driven to seek ordination to the priesthood so that, through the Eucharist, he could make possible the continued presence of Jesus with his people. Brother Charles felt a growing sense of urgency about carrying that awareness to others so that they might come to know the faith, peace, and joy that had been given to him.

Nazareth is not forever. A time came when Jesus felt driven to leave mother, kinfolk, and friends to forsake the home of his boyhood, the carpenter shop where he earned his living, and the familiar streets of the small town in which he had grown to manhood. That inner drive was the signal that his mission was beginning, a mission that meant abandoning the quiet life of a village craftsman for the discomfort, danger, and ultimate death involved in his public ministry.

A time also came when Brother Charles of Jesus had to shut the door of his hermit's shed and bring his message of hope to a world beset by doubt and despair.

In a sense, Nazareth would go with him. Whatever the future held, it would be built on the foundation stone of deliberately sought obscurity and close union with Jesus present on the altar under the appearance of bread. As he himself said, "May I live in Nazareth everywhere hidden with Jesus."

But the time had come for the man who had struggled in the darkness of disbelief for so long to witness to the gift he had been given. He put the exact description of his calling in the mouth of Jesus, imagining he was talking to him during a meditation: "Your vocation is to shout the Gospel from the rooftops, not in words, but with your life."

Step one in the mission was the priesthood, and in September 1900, he returned to France and reentered the Trappist Monastery of Our Lady of the Snows. Six months later, Charles de Foucauld, the French viscount whose life was so disgraceful that the French army had no place for him, was ordained a priest of God.

Step two was to find a "rooftop" from which to "shout the Gospel." And a strange rooftop it was—

for anyone except Charles de Foucauld. For four years he lived in Beni-Abbès, an obscure oasis in the northern Sahara. He spent his days providing hospitality to any who asked for it—French soldiers, Bedouins, the poor, the sick, the outcasts. He ministered to slaves in the caravans that passed, and knowing full well that neither he nor the slaves could do anything directly to alter their fate, he told them to seek strength and courage in prayer. At the same time, he wrote to his bishop and to powerful friends in France to take immediate steps to abolish the "monstrous immorality" of slavery. "We must shout out when we see evil," he told those who were in a position to do something about slavery in North Africa. By day, between scant hours snatched for sleep, Brother Charles of Jesus could be seen—except that there was no one to see him—on his knees before the altar, dwelling in obscurity with his Lord in a Nazareth that had become a state of mind rather than a geographical place. He was the only priest within a radius of 250 miles. And yet, by practical standards, he was one too many, since most of the time he was alone. He slept on the bare ground, ate only bread and boiled barley, and prayed.

Beni-Abbès was not isolated enough, however; and in 1905, Brother Charles of Jesus joined a caravan and headed south, a thousand miles farther into the desert. His destination was an even more obscure oasis, Tamanrasset. There he stayed, praying, imitating the "complete obscurity" of Jesus of Nazareth, and sharing his faith and his meager food with the few who passed his way. His hut, built with his own hands, was made of dirt and stone. It had two rooms, each smaller than a walk-in closet. Ta-manrasset's population consisted of forty dirt-poor laborers who scratched out a living from the sun-bleached soil of the oasis. It reminded Brother Charles of what Nazareth might have been like in the days when Jesus walked its streets.

Brother Charles had once imagined Jesus saying to him, "You must destroy in yourself everything that is not God. Make yourself a desert here, where you can be alone with me and listen to me as Mary Magdalen did." For Brother Charles, that desert was not the endless sand of the Algerian Sahara, it was his own solitude, his inner life of prayer and faith. In the desert, he felt safe and secure. Bitten by a snake, he refused to worry. He doctored the wound himself and shrugged it off with, "Jesus will take care of me." In illness, the response was the same—"God is there. He can help directly as well as through other people"—and when he was going deaf—"Deafness is a handicap hermits long for." Nothing was too painful or threatening to shatter the commitment of his faith.

Dead to the world, he no longer feared the death of the body. He had once written, "I should just love to go to Jesus soon," but as he became more deeply committed to shouting the Gospel with his life, he became more willing to stay as long as God had work for him to do. Since he had chosen to share the ob-scure life of Jesus at Nazareth, he was equally con-vinced that, in God's good time, he would share Je-sus' violent death. "My wish is to live as if I were to die a martyr today," he said in a variety of ways over the course of his life. Martyrdom did seek him out, for all was not sweetness and light in the real desert, the desert of outlaws and fugitives from justice, of armed nomads and rebels against the French occupation forces.

To some, Brother Charles of Jesus might have been a holy man who fed the hungry and ministered to the needs of the sick. He was also a Roman Catholic priest, an infidel in the eyes of the desert Muslims. And he was a Frenchman, hated by those on whom the yoke of colonial government rested heavily. On December 1, 1916, Brother Charles of Jesus was violently cut down near his hut in Tamanrasset. His killers were Senousis, radical terrorists who wanted to still his voice, hating as they did the religion he preached and the nation they thought he represented. And yet, in cutting down the grain of wheat, even in the isolation of the desert, the Senousis guaranteed a rich harvest.

Charles de Foucauld never made a convert. He never took in a disciple. He never built a church, school, or convent. Yet, today, in communities of the Little Brothers of Jesus and the Little Sisters of Jesus, his path to God through obscurity, worship, and service spreads and grows. In cities and in the desert, in slums and in poverty-ridden villages, his desire to serve the least of the brethren is still carried out. A rich harvest can be reaped from the deserts of this world, provided they are generously watered with the blood of heroes.

2.
Martin Luther
King, Jr.
Preacher

The slender black man sat alone at the kitchen table of the house on South Jackson Street in Montgomery, Alabama. He had been pastor of the Dexter Avenue Baptist Church for only three months, and someone had just threatened his life.

As he sat sipping coffee in the darkness of a December Alabama night, the young preacher thought of choices he had made. He realized that the calling he had chosen also involved the woman and child asleep in their rooms elsewhere in the house. He knew their lives would be shaped, perhaps shattered, by what he did, and he stared down the murky tunnel of the future, trying to see what it held for him, for them. He kept repeating to himself the words the caller had used, burned into his brain as by a branding iron: "Listen, nigger, we've taken all we want from you; before next week you'll be sorry you ever came to Montgomery."

He had known there would be a price to pay for trying to lead his people to greater freedom and dignity, for committing himself to make the American dream the black man's dream, too. Well, now it looked as if a down payment was already being demanded. Seated at that kitchen table in his parsonage, Martin Luther King, Jr., was sure of one thing—he was afraid. He was looking death in the face, and he had to make a decision that would put his life on the line every hour of every day for the rest of his life. He wondered whether he had the courage to do it. More exactly, he wondered whether he had the courage to practice the nonviolence he preached. He was convinced that the Gospel of Christian love and the nonviolent principles of Mohandas K. Gandhi and Henry David Thoreau could be welded together. He planned to use them to win equal treatment and equal opportunity for America's blacks.

Until September 1954, King had been preparing himself for the challenge, waging his campaigns mostly in his own head, in discussions with his wife, Coretta, or with sympathetic friends. After tonight, he would be waging it with such people as the anonymous caller who had just threatened him—all because of Rosa Parks.

Mrs. Parks was a seamstress at a big department store. She had also been secretary to the Montgomery branch of the National Association for the Advancement of Colored People, the NAACP. After working all day one Thursday, the forty-three-year-old woman had gone shopping, threading her way through the busy crowds of early Christmas shoppers in the unusually warm evening. A Cleveland Avenue bus pulled in, and Rosa Parks climbed aboard. The seats were filling rapidly, but she managed to get one in the row behind the section of the bus restricted to white passengers. She settled in with her bundles as the bus made its way through the busy city streets, and by the time it arrived in front of the Empire Theater, every seat was full.

Six white passengers boarded the packed bus, and the driver turned to the blacks sitting just behind the white section. "Let me have those seats," he said matter-of-factly. There was nothing unusual in what he did. It happened every day, all over the South, whenever the "whites only" seats were filled on a public bus. Used to such treatment, three blacks got up right away, but Rosa Parks stayed where she was. Her feet hurt. She had paid her fare, and she was going to stay in the seat she had taken when she boarded the bus. Again, the driver asked her to surrender her seat. Again, she refused.

That refusal triggered a spark that would change the history of the United States. It would also thrust Martin Luther King, Jr., onto the front pages of newspapers all over the world and, one day, it would cost him his life.

The bus driver called the police. Mrs. Parks was arrested. She was taken to jail, fingerprinted, and booked on charges of having broken Montgomery's segregation law. Others had refused before her. One black man had even been gunned down by a policeman for the same act. But in Rosa Parks's arrest, the black community found a person and an occasion to take a stand against the segregation that had dominated the South since the Civil War. Lincoln may have freed the slaves, but he could not make them equal or accepted. In the South, no black could eat at a white lunch counter, swim in a white pool, go to a white school, or ride in the white section of a bus. A host of other restrictions kept Southern blacks inferior long after they were technically freed by the Emancipation Proclamation. In the North, the unequal status was enforced more subtly, but just as effectively—until Rosa Parks refused to move.

Black leaders formed their plans to force Montgomery to integrate its bus lines, and even though he was such a recent arrival in the city, Martin Luther King, Jr., became more and more involved in the plans. While Dr. Ralph Abernathy handled the details of organizing the bus boycott, Dr. King mobilized the community. Young as he was in years, he was the best preacher, most suited to stir up the hearts and feelings of men, women, and children and to bring them together in common cause. Again and again, he stood on platforms and in pulpits explaining what the boycott was, what its goals were, and how they could be achieved.

Simply put, the boycott meant that black people in Montgomery would refuse to ride city buses on Monday, December 5, as a protest against Mrs. Parks's arrest. Dr. King asked black-owned taxi companies to cooperate with the boycott by carrying passengers for the ten-cent fare usually paid on the bus. Leaflets were distributed throughout black neighborhoods. On the Sunday before the target date, preachers at black churches urged their congregations to find other ways to get to work so that they could cooperate with the boycott.

Monday dawned. Martin and Coretta King set their alarm for 5:30 so that they could watch the 6:00 bus pass their house and see whether black people were observing the boycott. Many of the city's black domestics rode the early bus on the South Jackson line. It was usually packed. As the bus roared up, the Kings glanced anxiously out their window. The bus was empty. Fifteen minutes passed. The second bus of the day pulled up. It too was empty. The third bus went by. It had two passengers, both white. The boycott was working.

Dr. King jumped into his car and drove through the city, peering into bus windows, checking all bus stops. He counted only eight black people on buses that morning. Blacks had hitched rides, pooled cars, and walked. A few had even ridden mules. But almost unanimously, the black people of Montgomery had stayed off the buses.

On the day of the boycott, Mrs. Parks was tried and found guilty of disobeying the city's segregation law. She was fined fourteen dollars. Montgomery's black leaders replied by forming the Montgomery Improvement Association (MIA), and the man they chose to lead the new organization and to carry the boycott forward until equal treatment was won was Dr. Martin Luther King, Jr.

Montgomery was not his city. The boycott was not his idea, but the man and the moment were right. Martin King stepped onto the stage of history. He was twenty-six.

A mass meeting was called for that same night. Thousands gathered inside and outside the Holt

Street Church, eager to hear their leaders' plan of action. After a rousing chorus of "Onward Christian Soldiers," Dr. King stepped to the pulpit.

"We are tired," he said, "tired of being segregated and humiliated. We are impatient for justice. But we will protest with love. There will be no violence on our part. There will be no cross burnings. No white person will be taken from his home and murdered by a hooded Negro mob. If we do this, if we protest with love, future historians will have to say, 'There lived a great people, a black people, who injected new meaning and dignity into the veins of civilization.' "

The crowd roared their approval.

Dr. Abernathy took the microphone to outline the plan. He explained that city officials would be informed that no black would ride Montgomery's buses until (1) they were assured of courteous treatment by drivers; (2) passengers were seated on a first come, first served basis; (3) any seat anywhere in a bus could be taken by anyone, black or white; and (4) blacks were trained and hired to drive buses on all-black routes. He asked those who favored the plan to stand, and every man and woman in the church did so, raising their hands to make doubly sure their agreement was evident.

The boycott went forward. Support poured in from across the country and around the world. As the days turned into weeks, Martin Luther King, Jr., supplied the spark that kept people afire with the determination to persevere, to overcome. Always, he insisted that they remain nonviolent. "We must meet the forces of hate with the power of love," he told blacks throughout the city. "Above all, our aim must never be to defeat or humiliate the white man, but to win his friendship."

The right to preach that philosophy of nonviolence, of meeting hatred with love, was hard won. It had been solidified and, like steel, tempered on the night Martin Luther King, Jr., sat in his kitchen on South Jackson Street, confessing to himself and his God that he was afraid. Like most people, the young preacher was afraid—for himself, and for his wife and child—of violence and pain, of ridicule and abuse, of imprisonment and mockery. He was afraid of death. He knew that committing himself to work for the rights of his people might one day cost him his life, that it might even cost the lives of his family. He knew that he must embrace all those possibilities if he chose to go ahead as the leader of the MIA. As he sat and drank coffee, he prayed—aloud.

"I am taking a stand for what I believe is right," he told himself and God. "But now I am afraid. The people are looking to me for leadership, but I have no more courage."

Dr. King later described what happened next. He said that he became aware of an inner voice, a voice he was convinced came from God, and it told him, "Stand up for the right. I am with you."

Martin Luther King, Jr., would never be afraid again.

The first test of his newly born courage and faith took place three evenings later. Dr. King was out at a meeting. Mrs. King and another woman were watching television in the living room of the parsonage when they heard a thud on the front porch.

Mrs. King thought someone had thrown a brick at the house, but to be safe she and the other woman moved to the back part of the house, toward the nursery, where the Kings' infant daughter was sleeping. That decision saved their lives. A blast tore through the living room wall, breaking the front windows and filling the room with splinters of flying glass. Friends summoned Dr. King, and the young minister arrived home to find an angry mob of blacks, armed with knives, broken bottles, sticks, and rocks. They were ready for blood. All they wanted was his go-ahead.

Instead, the young preacher climbed on the smashed porch of the parsonage and gave the first proof that he was as willing to walk the walk of nonviolence as he was prepared to talk the talk about it.

"Get rid of your weapons," he shouted. "We must love our white brothers no matter what they do to us. What we are doing is just, and God is with us." Calmed, the crowd went home.

The work of the boycott went on. On November 13, 1956, nearly a year after Rosa Parks refused to move from her seat, the United States Supreme Court declared Alabama's state and local bus segregation laws to be in violation of the U.S. Constitution. On December 21, Dr. King and the Reverend Glenn Smiley, a white minister from New York, boarded the South Jackson Street bus. Together, they took a ride through the heart of Montgomery. History had been made—nonviolently.

In the next decade, Martin Luther King, Jr., would go on to other victories. He would engage in sit-ins, freedom marches, even wade-ins. He would serve time in jail. He would see others jailed, clubbed, attacked by tear gas and guard dogs, gunned down, and blown apart. He would stand on the steps of the Lincoln Memorial and tell America, black and white, of his dream, a dream of brotherhood and harmony, a dream of cooperation and unity. He would receive the Nobel Peace Prize for his dedication to nonviolence, and within two months, he would go from the auditorium of Oslo University to a jail cell in Selma, Alabama. Aware of the humor in his situation, he wrote from jail: "When the King of Norway participated in awarding the Nobel Peace Prize to me, he surely did not think that in less than sixty days I would be in jail."

Then he asked and answered the question that had motivated him throughout his ministry: "Why are we in jail? This is Selma, Alabama. There are more Negroes in jail with me than there are on the voting rolls."

Nonviolent protest—and the treatment it received—quickly made Selma a household word amidst a holocaust of pain and death. But the risks were not in vain. On August 6, 1965, President Lyndon B. Johnson signed the voting rights bill, giving blacks the vote in practice as well as in theory.

As the Vietnam conflict tore the United States apart, Dr. King saw that the war was being fought mostly by blacks and paid for with the money that was needed at home to defeat poverty. He denounced the war as "an enemy of the poor." Many of his supporters turned against him, accusing him of deserting his own people, of meddling in an affair that was none of his business, and of using Vietnam as a way of recapturing the publicity that younger, more radical leaders were taking away from him in the civil rights movement. He refused to change his position, convinced that nonviolence did not stop at the shores of the United States, that when violence was done to one human being, anywhere, all human beings had been violated.

As he was preparing another march on Washington, Dr. King was asked to lead protestors in a garbage collectors' strike in Memphis, Tennessee. As the strike dragged into its second month, the local clergy feared that mounting tensions between blacks and whites might explode. He went to Memphis and helped lay the groundwork for a city-wide work stoppage, a boycott by the black community. He promised to lead a march as part of the protest, and on April 3, 1964, he spoke at the Mason Street Temple.

"It is no longer a question of violence or nonviolence," he told the two thousand boycotters in the congregation. "It is nonviolence or nonexistence."

Then, almost as if he saw the future, he went on. He spoke of the many death threats he had received during his years as a civil rights activist. He explained that the plane he had just arrived on had been delayed because of a bomb scare.

"But it really doesn't matter with me now, because I've been to the mountaintop . . . I've looked over, and I've seen the Promised Land . . . I may not get there with you, but I want you to know that as a people we will get to the Promised Land . . ."

Dr. Martin Luther King, Jr., was right. He did

34

not live to get to the Promised Land, the land of his dream where black and white could live together in harmony. On Thursday, April 4, 1968, at one minute after six, as he chatted with his aides on the balcony of the Lorraine Motel in Memphis, an assassin's bullet snuffed out his life. He was thirty-nine years old.

3.
Saint
Brendan
The Navigator

"Good day to you, Father."

The old monk spun in his tracks to see the source of the piping voice that had surprised him on this deserted stretch of road. His twinkling eyes fell on a peasant lad, no more than ten or eleven years old, his rough wool tunic streaked with the dust of many hard-traveled miles. Thick brown hair stuck out in all directions from the top of the boy's head, and his moon of a face was split across the bottom into the broadest grin the monk had seen in many a day.

"And good day to you, lad," the monk boomed in a voice as deep as the breaking surf roaring shoreward not a half mile to their right. "Good day, indeed. Now what might a wee lad be doing wandering along the coast of Galway on this fine summer afternoon? Answer me that, if you don't mind, my good little sir."

"I'm off to the hill country beyond Annadown, Father, to mind my uncle's sheep. My cousin, his only son, has fallen ill, and there's no one to look after the flocks. I've been on the road for three days now, and I don't expect to arrive at my uncle's cottage for another two at least. And yourself, good Father. Where are you headed?"

The monk drew himself up to his full height, which must have been well over six feet. His brown monk's robe, which sported evidence of many years' patching and darning, hung loose and baggy on his sinewy frame. He stroked the thick curls of his beard. "It's not timid you are, my boy, coming right out and asking a total stranger, and a monk at that, where he's headed and what's his business." But before the boy could be frightened by the rebuke, the monk broke into another grin. "Well, since it's the Lord's business and nothing to be ashamed of, I'll tell you. I'm headed to Annadown myself—to the monastery founded there by the holy Saint Brendan. I'm a blacksmith, and old Brother Giles, who has been running the smithy at Annadown since Father Brendan first built the place, has finally gone home to God. I have been summoned to take his place. Just between you and me, boy, I think it's a bit of a waste of time. I'm going onto seventy-five myself, and I don't know how many more years the good monks can hope to get out of this old carcass. Oh well, that is not my problem, is it? As a monk, I obey the orders. Others give them."

At the mention of the Abbot Brendan, the young boy's face came alive. Everyone in Galway—for that matter, everyone in the West of Ireland—had heard wondrous tales of this holy monk—founder of many abbeys, traveler to far places, and worker of wonders. Only fifty years had passed since the great seafarer had returned from his last and most famous voyage. During the long winter nights, huddled over blazing peat fires, the men of Galway, brave seamen themselves in their frail leather curraghs, sat in their cottages spinning tale after tale about the adventures of the holy monk.

"You are old—" The lad stopped walking and speaking at the same instant as the tall monk's bushy eyebrows lowered into a deep frown over his blue eyes. "Forgive me, Father, I meant no offense. You told me just now that you are nearing seventy-five years. Saint Brendan, so my father says, died but fifty years ago. Perchance, did you know him?"

"Know him? Why, my lad, I was one of the seventeen monks he took with him on his final journey. Many were the marvels we saw, my boy, and frightful the dangers we faced. Had it not been for Father Brendan's holiness and courage, we would have perished or fallen into black despair more than once, I can tell you."

"Could you—would you tell me some of your adventures, good Father?" the boy asked, his eyes wide. "I have heard many tales about him of a winter's evening, but never from someone who actually shared the holy saint's journey."

"Bless me, I'll be happy to tell you our comings and goings, boy. A lad of your years can benefit a great deal from hearing the wonders God works and the great deeds his holy heroes can accomplish through faith in him and love for their fellows.

"It came about this way. Father Brendan was ruling over the monastery of Clonfert, not too far from here, and a busy man he was, with over three thousand monks on his hands. Well, who should show up one day but Saint Brendan's friend Abbot Barinth and a wonderful tale he had to tell.

"Abbot Barinth told of a visit he had made to the Paradise of the Saints, far off in the West, in company with a disciple of his named Mernoc who was abbot of a small monastery off the coast of Ireland. Brendan and Barinth talked far into the night, discussing where this wondrous place was and how to get there. Soon, nothing would do but that Father Brendan must voyage there and see the place for himself. As you know, boy, we Irish monks have been sailors for a long time. As our own Saint Columba has said, 'What joy to sail the crested sea.'

"Well, sail the crested sea we did. Father Brendan called us together one day, fourteen of us. He described his talks with Abbot Barinth, saying that he had heard rumors of such a place, but that Barinth had now convinced him of its existence. Father Brendan said he longed to sail there. 'Will you go with me, lads?' he asked.

"As one, we all said, 'Father Abbot, your will is our will. Have we not turned our backs on family and inheritance and placed our bodies in your hands? We are prepared to follow you to death, if God so wills.'

"Father Brendan was delighted, and we set to work building a big sailing curragh, large and sturdy enough to carry us to the Paradise of the Saints. We bound together a framework of oak and ash striplings, strong but flexible, so that they might ride gently on the sea. Sixty of the sturdiest oxen in all Galway were slain and their hides tanned with oak bark. Many nights and days did we sew those hides, stretching them over the curragh's sturdy frame, stitch by stitch. When that task was done, we took the grease we had made by boiling the flesh and bones of the oxen we had killed, and we caulked all the seams to make them tight against the seawater. Then we uprighted our fine boat and put in a small mast forward and a larger mast aft, each with a square woolen sail. We placed on board enough provisions for forty days, and she was ready to go.

"On the morn of our departure, Father Brendan said mass on the planks of the small deck we had built across the bow of the boat. Then, with much sprinkling of holy water and singing of psalms by the monks who were remaining behind, our little band made ready to put to sea. As we were hauling the boat into the surf, three monks raced down to the beach and pleaded with the holy abbot to take them along. He took them reluctantly, for Father Brendan knew the future, lad, and he told these latecomers that none of them would see Ireland again.

"At first, we had a beautiful following breeze and coasted merrily along in our sturdy craft. Then one day the breeze left us bobbing up and down on the oily-looking ocean swells, not a breath of air to fill our sails as they hung limp against the masts. Day after day we remained becalmed. We rowed all we could, but when the stores ran out, our strength faded. So, I regret to confess, did our faith and our courage. But not Father Brendan's, and he was just as hungry and thirsty as we seventeen crewmen. Nay, more so, since he had been sharing what little he had with one of the brethren who had fallen sick.

41

"Then we spotted a high rocky island, and we rowed as we had never rowed before. When we came within sight of the shore, our hearts sank like stones into the sea. Sheer rocky cliffs rose up from the ocean. The gray-green water rolled in enormous waves against massive boulders that would surely crush our frail curragh. No beach could we spy. More dead that alive, we slumped over our oars, convinced we would perish where we sat.

"'Brothers all, listen to me!' Father Brendan stood at the mainmast clutching his abbot's staff of office with his right hand and the ship's rigging with the other. 'God did not bring us this far in safety to let us perish within sight of land. Believe me, the good Lord will save us if we keep our faith in him. Within three days, I promise you, he will show us a harbor of refuge.'

"I've lived a long time, lad, and seen all kinds of men. But never have I beheld faith such as Father Brendan had during that first test of our little company. Believing in him more than in God (I'm ashamed to admit it, but it's the truth), we circled that stony island for three days. In vain did we look for a beach or ledge to land the curragh. Then, just before sunset on the third day, a dark shadow cast by the sun showed us a narrow split between the cliffs. Until the sun had hit from precisely that angle, it was completely hidden from us. We rowed for the opening, borne along on the breast of a giant comber, and shot into one of the prettiest little harbors I've ever seen.

"We beached the boat, a prayer of thanksgiving on our lips, when a small dog appeared from out of nowhere, yapping and frisking around Father Brendan as if the holy abbot had been his long-lost master. 'What a fine messenger the Lord has supplied,' said the Abbot. 'Let us follow him.'

"The pup led us to a deserted town where we found an immense castle. We entered and found the great hall bedecked with fine necklaces and silver. There was a table laden with bread and fish. We ate our fill and spent the night in the castle.

"As we slept, one of the three monks who had joined us at the last minute crept down into the great hall, stole a silver necklace, and hid it in the hood of his robe. Father Brendan had stayed in the hall throughout the night, praying in gratitude for our safe arrival. He spied the thief and made him return the necklace. As he heard the wretch's confession, wonder of wonders, out popped a wee devil from the monk's hood, cursing and yelling at Father Brendan for robbing him of a soul. The poor monk was so frightened that he took to bed and died that same night, having at least received the Lord's forgiveness at the hands of Father Brendan.

"Well, lad, the day grows late. We must soon stop and bed down among the bushes for the evening. I wish I could tell you all the marvels that befell us. We visited an isle where a wondrous flock of birds chanted the Holy Office, morning and evening. We once beached our boat on the back of a whale, but he shook us off and swam away as calm as you please. Father Brendan said the whale was the biggest creature that lived in the sea and that his name was Jasconius.

"We found one island that was filled to overflowing with giant sheep, and more than once, mysterious strangers fed and sheltered us.

"Another time, we came upon a small island on which lived a community of monks ruled over by an abbot named Ailbe. The monks said that every morning they found bread—the finest bread I have ever eaten, my boy—exactly enough for each day. The monks did not know who baked the bread or whence it came. They simply devoted themselves to chanting the hymns and psalms of the Holy Office each day of the year, and they trusted in God for their food.

"We sailed by a rocky island, as dead as dead could be, where no tree or grass bloomed on its hillsides. We wanted to land, but as we approached, the dome of the hills vomited smoke and fire, and huge burning rocks rained down around us. Believe me, we rowed away from that island as fast as we could and barely escaped with our lives.

"We hit storms the likes of which I never saw before and never hope to see again. Mountains of gray-green ocean towered over our vessel, threatening to bury her. Each time, the little curragh rode to the top like a cork on a pond, bouncing merrily over the worst seas the raging ocean could throw at her. But there was nothing merry about us monks. We were sick and frightened, wailing and calling on God to deliver us. All but Father Brendan. He sat calmly in the stern by the steersman, comforting and encouraging him, all the while ignoring the angry waves and howling wind.

" 'Father Brendan,' said I, climbing aft over the huddled bodies of the other monks, unable to contain myself after nearly a week of being pounded by the sea, 'have you no fear? What if our boat founders or breaks up under these waves?'

"The holy abbot looked at me, salt brine running in torrents down his long silky beard. He was about as old then as I am now. I don't mind telling you he was an impressive figure.

" 'Well,' says he, wiping seawater from his eyes, 'to be sure, brother, I am afraid of the might of the sea, just as you are. I too wonder if we have built our frail little ship well enough to survive this angry weather. But I keep my fear to myself. First, I know that the other monks take heart from my strength. As leader, it is my responsibility to hearten my brethren. Panic is a luxury I can ill afford if we are to come alive through this storm. Second, I claim to serve a loving, all-powerful God. To show fear would be to doubt the wisdom and the goodness of the Lord who has sent us on this journey and has now laid this test upon us to see if we are worthy of its happy conclusion. You and I both know, brother, that even though we must work as hard as we can in God's service, in the long run the results are in his hands. If he has brought us this far only to let us perish, then he has reasons of which we are ignorant. If he has decreed that we should reach the Paradise of the Saints, see it, and return to tell others so that his works may be glorified, then all the wind and water in the mighty ocean will not be able to sink our little boat.'

"Well, the storm ended, and we reached the Paradise of the Saints as had been foretold many times during our wanderings. A great fog swallowed our

45

boat as we approached, so that we could not see the bow from the stern. The steward from the Island of the Sheep, which we had revisited during our travels, had come along as our guide. He told Father Brendan that the Paradise of the Saints was eternally surrounded by fog, which was why few had ever found it. He told us how to sail, and within an hour of our entering the fogbank, we beheld a great light which guided us to the shore. What a sight greeted our travel-weary crew: a paradise it was, with endless daylight and trees bearing fruits sweeter than I have ever tasted.

"For forty days we wandered through this amazing land, until we reached a river so broad and deep we were afraid to cross. As if from thin air, a young man appeared on the shore and beckoned. We took heart and crossed the river without mishap. The young man sang psalms with us and told us that the Lord had kept us seven years on the ocean that we might see the great wonders of the western ocean. The young man said we were not to explore anymore, but we should take some of the fruits and precious stones from that place and return home, for the day of Father Brendan's death was not far off. He foretold that others would find the Paradise of the Saints at some future time, when Christians were being persecuted.

"We did as he instructed, and Father Brendan steered our little vessel through the fog and across the ocean back to Ireland. He made a visit to all his monasteries one last time, telling the brothers of the wonders he had seen. Then, the holy abbot took the last sacraments of Holy Mother Church and fell asleep in the Lord."

The old monk turned and took the young boy's hands in his. "Son, I have spent half a century wondering what God's purpose was in bringing us on that voyage. None has been brave enough to try such a journey since the holy abbot Brendan was laid in his grave. Surely, I could never have found the courage in my heart to undertake such a venture. After many years of prayer and thought, I now know the answer: God calls some people to push out into unknown places, to do dangerous things, or to think daring ideas so that the rest of us, the ordinary folk, will always be aware that there is a new horizon to seek, a new hill to climb. Because they took risks, we are reminded to be just a little better than we might otherwise be."

The old monk grabbed the lad's arm and headed for the side of the road. "Come, lad, it's time to take a bite to eat and have a bit of sleep. We've got a long walk ahead of us tomorrow."

4.
Sir Thomas More

Reluctant Hero

The old man looked up from his writing as the clank of armor echoed faintly across the courtyard in the early-morning light. Perhaps they are bringing word that the time for my execution has been set, he thought, almost as if he were speculating about the weather that day. Death beneath the headsman's ax held little fear for Sir Thomas More. He had lived with death for a long time. For almost fourteen months he had been a prisoner in the Tower of London, and he had watched others go forth to meet their deaths for believing as he did. He knew full well that, depending on the whim of the king, he might be next. The summons would come one day, if not today, and he would go as bravely as he knew how to rendezvous with the ax. If his courage faltered, then God must help him.

Thomas More, the most brilliant lawyer in England during an age noted for brilliance, was a realist above all else. He did not deal in guesses or wishes. His life had been devoted to facts, to evidence, to seeking to know and enforce the clear meaning of the king's law.

Sir Thomas had been a realist when he had reluctantly agreed to serve Henry VIII as lord Chancellor—a combined secretary of state and chief justice of the Supreme Court—the highest position of honor the king could bestow. Next to the king, the lord chancellor was the most powerful man in England.

All of More's predecessors were men of the church, more than one of them cardinals, and many had used the office to gain wealth and power for themselves, their relatives, and their friends. But Thomas More was realistic enough to know that the office had been given at the king's pleasure and could as easily be taken away. So Sir Thomas had vowed that when the time came he would leave office with clean hands, and he took nothing for himself or anyone else. A commoner, he had neither an acquired nor an inherited fortune, and he had put down the chancellorship no richer than he was when he had taken it up. It was well that he had done so, for in trying to find grounds to condemn him, Sir Thomas' enemies had tried to prove that his hands were as soiled as those of every other magistrate in England.

The ex-chancellor chuckled and stroked his long gray beard as he recalled an occasion when his prosecutors had been undone by their own cunning. King Henry, impatient over Sir Thomas's refusal to support his divorce from Queen Catharine, had requested the King's Counsel to summon More on a charge of bribe taking. Thomas Boleyn, earl of Wiltshire, father of Anne Boleyn, the king's new queen and second wife, demanded to know if it were not true that Sir Thomas More had accepted an expensive cup from the wife of one Master Vaughan, a man in whose favor Sir Thomas had decided a case.

Yes, the former chancellor admitted, he had taken the cup, a long time after handing down the decision in Master Vaughan's favor. Mistress Vaughan had brought it to his house on New Year's Day as a gift, and she was so insistent, More told the counsel, that out of courtesy he could not refuse it.

The earl of Wiltshire jumped to his feet. "Did I not tell you, my lords, that you should find this charge to be true?" he clucked like a hen that has just laid an exceptionally large egg.

Sir Thomas More waited calmly until the counsel members finished congratulating each other for having found him out so quickly. Then he raised a hand for attention. "My lords," he said quietly, "you have heard me tell the first half of the tale. Perhaps it is not seeking too much to have your attention for the second half as well.

"Yes, I did take the gilt cup. I had my butler fill it with wine, and I drank a New Year's toast to Mistress Vaughan." The lords beamed at one another, delighted to find the supposedly brilliant lawyer immersing himself deeper and deeper in guilt.

"I had the butler refill the cup, handed it to the good woman, and she drank a toast to me. Then, much against her will, I demanded that she take the cup back to her husband as his New Year's gift from me."

The silence had been thunderous, Sir Thomas recalled with a smile, as Thomas Boleyn and his fellow counselors watched their case dissolve into thin air. It was well, indeed, the ex-chancellor thought, that he had not turned his office into a means of gaining wealth or favor for himself or those close to him, for he would quickly have sealed his doom by such dishonesty.

But he had not taken the post for himself; he had taken it to serve God, king, and country. And when that was no longer possible, he had put down the office as readily as he had taken it up. Even as he accepted the heavy gold chain that was the symbol of his rank, the realist in Sir Thomas knew that his actual burdens would be much heavier: he must try to keep the king from dividing the nation over his divorce; he must be a discreet ally to poor Queen Catharine; he must stop Henry from reducing England to beggary through costly foreign wars; and he must be very, very cautious.

Sir Thomas had been under no illusion about the fragility of the king's favor. When he was under-treasurer, largely responsible for raising funds to support Henry's European military adventures, the king had unexpectedly visited More's house in Chelsea. After dinner, Henry had strolled in Sir Thomas's garden, an arm thrown affectionately around his host's shoulder.

William Roper, More's son-in-law, later pointed out what a sign of royal favor such a gesture was. "I have never seen him do that to anyone else," he said, "although he did once walk arm in arm with Cardinal Wolsey."

"I thank God, son," the older man had replied,

"that the king is so friendly to me. But don't put too much faith in such signs of affection. If my severed head would win him a castle in France, it should not fail to go."

Sitting in his cell, aware that the king's messengers might even now be on their way to announce the time of his execution, Sir Thomas thought ruefully just how prophetic he had been. Cardinal Wolsey, with whom the king had walked arm in arm, was dead, stripped of his office in disgrace. On his way to a trial that would surely have resulted in a death sentence, Wolsey had robbed the executioner of a victim by succumbing to age and sickness. And now, thought Sir Thomas, I, his successor as lord chancellor, await my own execution.

Not that Sir Thomas regretted the decisions that had brought him to this place. He had foreseen the possibility from the outset. He had not become chancellor to spare himself. He had done so to serve his king, and he had done his best to administer justice fairly and to counsel the king wisely. On the subjects of the king's marriage and his supremacy over the Church of England, More had maintained a stony silence.

Sir Thomas took legitimate pride in some of his achievements as chancellor. His court had been honest and fair. William Roper had once complained that being More's son-in-law had produced no benefit for him.

Sir Thomas said he would do all he could to help his kinsman. "But I assure you of one thing," he told Roper, "if the parties in a case call for justice, then even if my own father stood on one side and the devil on the other, the devil should win the decision if his case was just."

Justice in Sir Thomas's court was also swift, something almost unknown in England at that time, for when he became lord chancellor, some cases had been waiting to come to trial for twenty years. Before he resigned, the court calendar was vacant. One day, Sir Thomas called for the next case, only to be told by the clerk that there was no case waiting to be heard. "Thanks be to God," the lord chancellor had replied, "that for once this busy tribunal is at rest."

The burdens of office, however, took their toll on Sir Thomas. So did the pressure put on by the king to come out publicly in favor of his divorce and to recognize, as the clergy and the House of Commons had already done, that Henry was "their singular protector, only and supreme Lord, and so far as the law of Christ allows, even Supreme Head" of the Church of England.

More could not make that declaration, and it would cost him his head.

Thomas More did not spend his time as chancellor brooding over how bad things were. He was a merry individual, and there had been many an occasion for merriment. Sir Thomas recalled an incident involving his wife's pet dog. Dame Alice More loved little dogs, and unknown to her, someone had given her a pup that had been stolen from a beggar woman. The beggar spotted the dog being carried by one of Dame Alice's servants and came before Sir Thomas demanding that the puppy be returned. In the face of Dame Alice's protest—with equal force—that the dog belonged to her, Sir Thomas recalled how King Solomon had decided a case involving two women, each of whom claimed to be the mother of the same baby. Knowing that the real mother would rather see her child go to another woman than see it dead, Solomon threatened to cut the child in two, giving each mother half a baby.

The lord chancellor decided to imitate the wise ruler of ancient Israel, and he had his wife, the beggar, and the mongrel brought before him.

"Wife, stand at the upper end of the hall," he said. "Woman," he told the beggar, "you stand at the other end."

Then he stood between the two women, holding the dog. "Are you willing to let me decide your dispute?" he asked. They said they would accept his decision.

Sir Thomas put the dog on the floor and told both women to call it, explaining that whichever woman the pup obeyed was obviously the rightful owner.

The dog went to the beggar woman, leaving Sir Thomas with another problem, a greatly upset wife. This he solved by giving the beggar a gold coin and buying the dog back for Dame Alice. The incident had ended happily for all and provided many a good chuckle in the More household. And, thought Sir Thomas, smiling to himself now in his cell in the tower, I came as close to the wisdom of Solomon as I am ever likely to get in this world.

Coming out of his reverie, Sir Thomas realized that it had been some time since he had heard the rattle of armor from the other side of the courtyard. Perhaps the king's summons had arrived for some other wretch. Or perhaps it was routine tower business. If the message was for him, the bearer of the king's words was certainly in no hurry to deliver them.

A loud rap on the door of his cell interrupted his thoughts. The heavy oak door swung slowly open, revealing Sir Thomas's good friend, Thomas Pope, wearing a sadder face than the former lord chancellor had seen in many a day. He needed no words from the young man to explain why he was so sad. Obviously, the time had come. The king had been kind to let young Pope convey the news, knowing that he would do so gently.

"Thank you, Master Pope," Sir Thomas said after his friend told him that he was to die before nine o'clock that very morning. He also thanked the king, in the person of his messenger, for all the kindnesses his sovereign had done him. In his list of kindnesses, Sir Thomas included the leisure resulting from his confinement, which had allowed him time to draw closer to the God he was soon to meet, and even the royal decision "so shortly to rid me of the miseries of this wretched world."

Master Pope held up a hand, interrupting his friend. "The king's pleasure is further," he said, "that at your execution you shall not use many words."

Henry was asking his former chancellor to forgo the custom of giving a long speech from the scaffold, in which he would tell what had brought him to this place of death and argue one last time the rights and wrongs of his case. The king was taking no chances that the most powerful opponent to his divorce and to his being named head of the Church of England would stir up trouble during his last moments on earth.

More agreed to the request, asking only that his daughter Margaret be allowed to attend the execution. Pope explained that the king had already given permission for Dame Alice and More's children to attend. Then he burst into tears. Sir Thomas found himself in the odd position of consoling the man who had just delivered his death sentence.

"Quiet yourself, good Master Pope," he told the young man, "and be not discomforted; for I trust that we shall, once in Heaven, see each other full merrily, and we shall be sure to live and love together in joyful bliss eternally."

Sir Thomas had but a few hours to prepare himself for death, so Thomas Pope and the guards respectfully withdrew.

Did Sir Thomas More review the details of his conflict with his king during those final hours? Did he use the time for prayer and reflection, seeking help to keep his courage firm so that he would not betray on the scaffold the beliefs for which he had suffered thus far? No one can know what passed through his mind.

Perhaps he recalled how he had done all in his power to avoid speaking out on the question of Henry's divorce. He had kept silent, knowing the king would obtain the divorce anyway. Those who opposed him might slow things up, but sooner or later they would be crushed or won over to Henry's will.

Sir Thomas knew he could never side with the

king. And he was reluctant to be a martyr. So he kept his opinion to himself as long as he could. As a shrewd realist, he also knew that silence would never satisfy Henry, for in More's refusal to take a stand the king saw a silent condemnation.

The prosecutor at Sir Thomas's trial had charged that silence on the question of the king's supremacy over the Church convicted More of maliciously and traitorously depriving the king of a title bestowed on him by both the House of Commons and the clergy. Sir Thomas had vehemently rejected the charge, arguing that treason was to be found in words or deeds, not in silence.

"For my silence," he had reminded his judges, "neither your law nor any law in the world is able justly and rightly to punish me."

He then argued for freedom of conscience, saying, "You must understand that in things touching conscience, every true and good subject is more bound to have respect to his own conscience and to his soul than to any other thing in all the world," and he reminded the judges that he had not disclosed his views on the king's marriage or the legitimacy of his claim to be head of the church "to any person living in all the world."

But even as he was presenting his defense, Sir Thomas realized that logic and justice had no place in a court that had reached its verdict—his guilt—before it had begun to hear evidence. That he would die was a foregone conclusion. His judges might sleep easier and justify their action to a watching nation and world if they could produce the evidence to support a death sentence. But whether they did so or not, Sir Thomas More's head would fall.

Of one thing Sir Thomas could be positive: he had done all in his power to avoid a showdown. He did not want to be a martyr. Not that he doubted the truths for which he was condemned. No, Thomas More did not doubt that marriage was sacred or that the Church could have only one visible head. He sought to avoid martyrdom because he doubted his own courage. He could not be certain that he would be able to overcome his fear of torture or death. He was afraid he might fail such a test, so he did all in his power to avoid being condemned. If his efforts failed, why then, it must be God's will that he die on the scaffold. And if it were God's will, God would surely strengthen him in his hour of trial.

A soft knock at the door of his cell told him that it was time. Sir Thomas rose, picked up a small cross, followed the lieutenant of the guard out of the tower, and walked the few hundred yards to the site of his execution. The long months in prison had weakened Sir Thomas, so that he looked worn and aged, but suffering had not lessened his sense of humor. Afraid that he might stumble as he climbed the stairs to the scaffold, he said to the lieutenant, "I pray you, master lieutenant, see me safe up, and for my coming down let me shift for myself."

Then the most famous man in King Henry's England, save for the king himself, gave a speech, keeping it brief as his sovereign had requested. He asked the bystanders to pray for him, and he promised that he would pray for them after his death. He begged them to pray for the king, especially that God should give him good counselors.

Then came the words that would echo down the centuries: "I die," said Sir Thomas More, "the king's good servant, but God's first." This was the central issue, the one point he could not, in good conscience, yield.

Then he knelt and placed his neck on the block, and in a swift blur the executioner's ax struck down.

A reluctant hero, an unwilling martyr, Sir—now Saint—Thomas More had often prayed, "May we meet merrily in Heaven."

5.

Damien
de Veuster

Leper

Damien de Veuster hummed softly as he splashed cold water over his face and arms. "Ave, Maris Stella . . . Hail, Star of the Sea." The familiar words of the ancient Latin hymn in praise of the Mother of Jesus seemed particularly fitting there in the rose-tinted tropical morning of Molokai. "Hail, Star of the Sea, our life, our sweetness, and our hope . . ."

The comforting refrain from the Morning Prayer died on the priest's lips as his glance focused on the skin of his right arm. Gray Spots. Yellowish gray. He touched them. Dry, almost scaly. His stomach muscles clenched as the awareness invaded his consciousness, numbing his mind: Leprosy! Those innocent-looking spots were an early sign of leprosy! They would become larger, more numerous, like deadly freckles consuming and replacing the healthy tissue. They would destroy his sense of feeling. Then, beneath the speckled skin, would form the leprous tubercles, small hard lumps in which leprosy would fester and grow, spread through his body, eating muscle and bone, building its strength by consuming his. Thirty-six years old, a constitution like an ox; nonetheless, a leper. Damien shuddered as the image sank into his brain.

What was it he had written his brother? "I am not a leper yet, and with the miraculous help of God and the Blessed Virgin, I never will be." That had been but a few months after his arrival. With his young, strong body, his heart flushed with the heroism of the gesture he was making, Damien had found such bravado easy. Well, the miracle had lasted three years. Maybe three years was all he had a right to expect, perhaps more than he had a right to claim. After all, the Lord gave miracles only where nothing else would serve his will. Why should a priest who had volunteered to live among lepers expect to be anything but a leper himself? Wasn't the missioner's rule of conduct "like to like"? Or, as Saint Paul had put it, to become "all things to all men"?

Leprosy had been inevitable, Damien now knew. In fact, he had known his fate when he first stepped onto the coral sand of Molokai. In a secret corner of his heart, where he had never dared allow himself to look, was the knowledge that one day he would share the affliction of his people, just as surely as he had volunteered to share their exile.

Damien had embraced the possibility of leprosy when he offered to join the lepers, the unwanted ones, in the government preserve on Molokai. That day three years ago, he had offered God an open-ended commitment. Today, that pledge had been called in. The miracle was over. Damien de Veuster would not be numbered among those described in the Bible who would demonstrate God's power by walking unharmed among the asp and the adder, who would drink poison and not feel its deadly effects. But one day, as the gray spots slowly bore their deadly fruit, another biblical image would fit him better: "I am a worm and not a man, a shame to mankind, and despised of the people."

An outcast by choice when he came to Molokai, he would soon be an outcast by law, forbidden by the government of Hawaii to leave the settlement and bring his dreaded disease among civilized men.

Well, he thought in his simple peasant's way, I will have good company, I will be following a good example. Had not that very psalm been applied to the Savior, who had also chosen to be cast out and rejected by men? Was not Damien's commitment in becoming a priest an expression of willingness to follow the Lord all the way to Calvary if called to do so? Had he not taken an even more radical step in volunteering to take his brother Pamphile's place on the mission to Hawaii when Pamphile had been stricken with typhus? And did he not seal that commitment by offering to work among the lepers? If he ever thought commitments could be taken lightly, Damien now knew that what you offered, you could expect to have accepted in the most unlikely circumstances.

Damien strolled to the veranda of his second-floor living quarters and looked down on the cemetery spread out below. His thick peasant's hands, fingernails chipped and broken from shoveling dirt and manhandling rocks and lumber to build houses, chapels, and clinics, gripped hard at the rough wooden rail.

One day, perhaps soon, I, too, shall lie here among my people, a leper among lepers, he thought. He fought the tears that the pain in his soul was forcing into his eyes, and he wrestled with the sense of abandonment that was trying to smother him. There will be a difference, he reminded himself, gaining control. These people were forced to come here, hunted and driven by the government and the white citizens of Hawaii. I am here of my own will, a volunteer living out a borrowed vocation undertaken for a sick brother. I asked for this by everything I have done in my life. Can I refuse to accept what I have so ardently pursued?

Ten years earlier, Damien recalled, he had demanded of his superiors, "Let me take his place." Was it only ten years? The gulf separating the lush beauty of Molokai and its hidden blight of leprosy from the monastic headquarters of the Sacred Hearts Fathers on Rue Picpus in Paris seemed so vast, those words might have been spoken on another planet, an eternity ago.

Damien was born Joseph de Veuster in Tremeloo, Belgium, in 1840. He was the youngest son, the seventh of eight children born to Frans and Anne Catherine de Veuster.

Frans was a farmer who made a decent living out of the fertile Belgian soil and who probably worked a lot harder at his farming than he did at the Catholic faith into which he had been born along with just about everyone else in Tremeloo.

Joseph's mother was the religious one in the family, drilling into her children the truths of their catechism, hovering over them as they recited their prayers, and reading her wide-eyed brood the lives of the saints from an enormous volume that had been in the de Veuster family many years.

Two sisters and a brother, August, who would be known in religion as Pamphile, went off to serve the church full time, but no one ever expected or intended that little Joseph should become a priest. At thirteen, he had been withdrawn from school by his father and put to work on the family farm. His solid body thrived on the work, and he quickly became a good farmer, although the life of the soil seemed to leave his mind and soul unsatisfied. When Joseph turned eighteen, his father decided he should return to school. Time spent acquiring some business knowledge would keep his brain occupied and also make him a shrewder grain trader when his time came to sell the produce at local markets.

Away from the family nest, given a small taste of what might be his, the young farmer soon developed other plans. He wrote his parents a letter in which he pointed out how his sisters and brother had been able to follow the calling they felt toward religious life. "I hope," he told his father and mother, "my turn will come."

No one seems to have taken him too seriously at first, although his father did give permission for the lad to spend some time with his brother Pamphile at the Monastery of the Sacred Hearts Fathers in Louvain, Belgium. The reasons for the stay, Frans made clear, was so that Joseph might learn more French, which would make him an even more effective trader come market time.

Joseph learned French, but the market was never to reap the fruits of his studies. Within six months after his stay at Louvain, he informed his parents that he had reached the decision to dedicate himself to God. He planned on becoming a Trappist monk. The hard life of the cloister, with its fasts, long hours of prayer, and hard manual labor, probably struck him as a good way to take his life as a peasant farmer and build of it a fitting temple for God's service. But Pamphile pushed the merits of his own order and convinced his young brother that service in the Congregation of the Sacred Hearts of Jesus and Mary would be just as pleasing to the Lord and would have the added benefit of keeping the two brothers together. Joseph, soon to be renamed Damien after an early Christian missionary and physician, joined his brother at Louvain.

At first, no one thought of considering Damien for the priesthood. His methodical farmer's mind and his stolid peasant's outlook seemed better suited for the role of choir brother. He would join those assigned such tasks as chanting the Divine Office, caring for the buildings and grounds of the monasteries, and nursing the sick members of the community. Damien had only a workaday knowledge of French, the congregation's official language, and he knew absolutely no Greek or Latin, the language in which the priests of the order were trained in philosophy and theology. The priesthood was not for young Damien de Veuster.

Damien, however, had other plans. He may have been simply educated, but he was not simple-minded. His intellect was not like Pamphile's, swift and subtle, a rapier able to parry and thrust among the fine points of philosophy and theology, but Damien was a plodder. Like a good Belgian farm horse, he was built for distance, not speed; still, he got where he wanted to go in his own time and in his own way. Pamphile agreed to coach him, and Damien eventually convinced his superiors that he could master the languages of scholarship and that he could put those languages, once mastered, to work wrestling with the concepts of sacred theology. He thrived on the discipline and prayer life of the order, and his physical vitality and spiritual joy sometimes burst into such laughter and happiness that Pamphile, the serious scholar, felt obliged to caution his brother to dampen his enthusiasm.

Early in his religious life, Damien decided to be a missioner. Where he might serve would depend on his superiors' acceptance of his offer and their decision about where his talents might best fit the society's needs.

Meanwhile, Pamphile had been ordained a priest and assigned to Hawaii. On October 23, 1863, Pamphile and five other Sacred Hearts priests and brothers would sail for the Pacific islands, probably never to see Europe or loved ones again. Damien, the would-be missioner with the iron constitution and boundless energy, seemed fated to stay behind to finish his studies, while Pamphile, the quiet intellectual, sailed off to the arduous life of a missionary.

As the poet said, "God writes straight with crooked lines." Pamphile came down with a severe case of typhus while ministering to the sick during an epidemic that hit Paris just a few weeks before his departure. It was obvious that he would never recover in time to sail.

The question in everyone's mind was, who would take his place? Damien asked it. With more daring than tact, he went over the head of his immediate superior and asked the father general of the order if he might not replace Pamphile. The request was unusual, not only because it ignored the chain of command, but because Damien was not even ordained a priest. He would require several more years of theological studies before the honor of the priesthood would be his. Yet something in the young man's enthusiasm must have impressed the father general, because Damien was named to fill the vacancy. Ordination to the priesthood could take place in Hawaii, the superior decided, when Damien had satisfied the authorities there that he was ready for it.

As soon as the father general's letter arrived, Damien rushed to his brother's sickroom, jumping and shouting for joy. "I am going in your place! I am going in your place!"

Perhaps the older brother felt a pang of envy or regret, maybe even anger, at his brother's lack of tact. Maybe he felt relieved, for nothing in Pamphile's later life gave any indication that he would have been an effective missionary. His was to be a priesthood of lecture halls and scholarly books, not of slogging along narrow mountain trails in tropical downpours or enduring the stink and horror of the leper colony.

After Damien's death, Pamphile would be assigned to Molokai in the hope that one brother might carry on the other's high calling. Pamphile would do his best for a year, but he would fail miserably, and with his superior's reluctant consent return to Louvain to live out the remaining years of his life, faithful to Damien's memory, but incapable of walking in his footsteps.

Those events were in the dim future, however, impossible for Damien to see as he skipped around his brother's sickbed chanting, "I am going in your place!"

What he did see was a calling to heroism—although he would have blushed at the term—an opportunity to choose a kind of martyrdom. First, he would be asked to die to family, friends, and homeland. Then, he would be asked to accept death itself, slow, putrid, stinking death, as an outcast among outcasts. Each time, his answer would be an unquestioning yes.

To be a farmer is to know the cycles of life, its times of birth, growth, and death. To be a peasant is to live close to those rhythms, to see the world in straightforward terms. When he took his vows in the Sacred Hearts congregation, Joseph had stretched on the chapel floor, covered by a purple shroud, a burial garment. He had arisen, no longer Joseph, but Damien. Thinking the way a peasant and farmer thinks, he had perhaps taken that "little death" more literally than most of his fellow religious. If so, he had shown more wisdom—and more heroism—than they would probably have considered a young farm boy capable of demonstrating.

Damien de Veuster, Damien the Leper as the world came to know him even before his death, lived another fifteen years after that first horrifying morning when he detected on his body the telltale signs of leprosy. By the time of his death, Monday in Holy Week, April 15, 1889, at eight o'clock in the morning, he was world famous. He also experienced as much emotional and mental anguish as he did physical pain from the disease eating away at his body, for as his fame spread, Damien's superiors accused him of seeking his own glory. He begged for another priest to share his exile so that he might have someone to confess to, but his pleas were ignored. He demanded more money to build houses and buy medicines for his lepers, but his superiors told him to learn humility. And as a world ever in need of heroes elevated Damien on the altar of public acclaim, his fellow religious questioned his integrity and challenged his motives.

Eventually, others joined Damien in his exile, but none caught the world's imagination as he had, and the doomed priest continued to burn himself out, building for his lepers, recruiting people to carry on his work after he was gone, coaxing the government to be even more generous with money, food, medicine, and clothing. He went on doing what he had always done, doing the best he knew, and paying the price in the slow decay of his body for the opportunity he had requested as a young man of eighteen when he had asked his parents, "When will it be my turn?"

The details of the future were hidden from Damien on the day he first realized that he had become a leper. But he knew what the disease would eventually demand of him. That awareness gave a new soul-wrenching meaning to the words he always used to open his sermon at the morning mass for the leprous exiles of Molokai.

As was his custom, but aware to the roots of his soul of his new identity, the physical unity that had been forged between him and his congregation that day, Damien turned from the altar, his rugged farmer's body scarcely concealed by the well-worn priestly vestments, and said,

"My fellow lepers . . ."

6.
Bill W.

Alcoholic

The man pacing the lobby of Akron, Ohio's May-flower Hotel was tall and thin. He appeared to be in his mid-thirties, and he was obviously worried. His long legs carried him back and forth from the bar entrance at one end of the lobby to the church directory on the opposite wall. It was Saturday, the day before Mother's Day, 1935, and an early-evening crowd was beginning to fill the little hotel bar. Their happy chatter and the rattle of ice in cocktail glasses reached him through the bar's open doorway.

Bill W. was an ex-stockbroker who had come from New York with a group of businessmen who were hoping to take over a small company that made machine tools. The New Yorkers had lost the opening battle for control of the company, and the others had returned home. Bill had stayed behind to keep an eye on things while they tried to round up more money from their Wall Street contacts. Bill was alone in Akron with ten dollars in his pocket.

Shortness of funds, however, was not what was making him nervous. Each time Bill's pacing brought him to the door of the bar, he looked anxiously—and longingly—inside at the people enjoying their evening cocktails. He thought of the soft lights, the pleasant conversation, the shining crystal, and the bracing flavor of good liquor. He especially thought of the liquor. He felt he could taste it as he stood in the doorway. He wanted a drink more than almost anything else in the world, yet he knew he could not safely have one. He was an alcoholic, a man whose life had more than once been turned into a shambles because he could no longer handle alcohol. He had squandered large amounts of money on drinking, lost thousands of dollars because of bad decisions made while drunk or during a hangover. He had been hospitalized more than once because of his drinking, only to return to the bottle. Each time his drinking became worse and the recovery took longer.

Bill knew that alcohol was out of the question. For him, to drink would eventually mean insanity or death. His doctor had assured him that one or the other of these results would occur, sooner rather than later, if he picked up another drink. Yet, as he paced, the craving for alcohol set his nerves on edge, and the desire to join those people in the hotel bar became more and more desperate.

Bill's steps led him back to the church directory. He stared blankly at the list of churches in the city of Akron, unable to shake the conviction that he was about to get drunk once again. His mind started playing tricks on him. It told him that he didn't have to get drunk, that he could go into the bar, climb onto a stool, and order a ginger ale.

What I really want, he lied to himself, is just a

chance to strike up an acquaintance with someone and enjoy a little pleasant conversation.

But then the truth hit Bill like a runaway locomotive: he knew that what he really wanted was not a casual friendship or a quiet conversation. He wanted a drink, lots of drinks; his body was screaming for alcohol. He couldn't drive the thought of it from his mind.

As he stood staring at the bulletin board without really focusing on the names of the churches, Bill thought back to the preceding December.

His old friend, Ebby, a school pal and drinking buddy, had appeared out of nowhere at Bill's house in Brooklyn. Ebby looked bright and happy, and he was sober.

Ebby—who had always been a much worse drinker than Bill—explained that he had found a way to stay away from drinking. He had joined up with a small group of Christians, called the Oxford Group, who had shown him their simple guidelines for living a decent life: to admit that he was powerless over his drinking problem; to take a good look at himself by taking inventory of his strengths and weaknesses; to admit his shortcomings to another human being he could trust; and to make amends for his past life, including paying back what he had borrowed or stolen.

Ebby said that the Oxford people had told him to find an understanding of God that meant something to him, a belief in a higher power to whom he could commit himself. They said he should pray to that God for help in straightening out his life.

Ebby had smilingly sat at Bill's kitchen table, sipping coffee, and told his former drinking companion that this kind of religion had worked for him. He no longer had to drink.

As Ebby spoke, Bill realized that his friend was getting through to him in a way that no one else had ever been able to—not his wife, his family, Doctor Silkworth, various bosses, even good friends.

"In the kinship of common suffering," Bill later wrote, "one alcoholic had been talking to another," and that was the key difference between Ebby's words and all the lectures and scoldings Bill had heard over the years. One alcoholic talking to another.

Bill was convinced enough to give Ebby's suggestion a try, although the thought of all that religion made him uncomfortable. He made sure he had downed a few beers before taking himself off to an Oxford Group meeting with his former drinking buddy. To Bill's surprise, the Oxford approach worked, although it took him a few days to get completely sober. For three days after that first meeting, Bill wandered around, drinking and drunk most of the time. The awareness slowly took hold of him that his sickness could be treated if he could follow the course of recovery the Oxford people suggested: admit defeat; take stock of yourself; confess to a trusted person; make amends to those you have harmed; and pray for help to God as you understand him.

Confused as he was, Bill realized that the best way for him to start the healing process would be to check into a hospital and get the alcohol out of his system. Back he went to his friend, Dr. William D. Silkworth, at Towns Hospital in New York City. The good doctor winced to see Bill show up once again, drunk and in need of drying out, promising that he had at last found the answer, that he would never have to drink again. Dr. Silkworth put Bill in a private room and prescribed sedatives to help him come off the drinking spree.

While Bill was in his room shaking the alcohol out of his system, his wife, Lois, was in Dr. Silkworth's office looking for a ray of hope. The kindly doctor had no hope to give her. He sadly shook his head and explained that Bill was enslaved by alcohol, that it had literally made him insane, and that, since he could not seem to stop drinking, sooner or later he might have to be placed in a mental institution, if the alcohol didn't kill him first.

After a few days, Bill was taken off the sedative prescribed for his shakes. Physically, he was getting better, but mentally and spiritually, he was getting worse by the hour. He was sunk in a depression, unable to see a glimmer of hope on the horizon.

One day, his depression changed to anger when he looked up and saw Ebby standing in the doorway with a big grin on his face. Furious that his friend was so happy when he was so full of self-pity, Bill asked Ebby, "What'd you say about a neat little formula?"

Ebby quietly repeated the guidelines he had learned at the Oxford meetings. He told Bill to find a God he could turn to and to pray to that God. He chatted a little while, and then he headed down the hall.

Bill's mood went from bad to worse. His depression became blacker and blacker. He weighed the things Ebby had told him, but each time the thought of praying entered his mind, he almost gagged. Then, suddenly, every shred of hope and self-respect, every trace of pride and stubbornness seem to drain from him. His ego seemed to be wiped out, completely deflated. Before he knew what was happening, Bill heard himself cry out, "If there is a God, let him show himself! I am ready to do anything, anything!"

At that moment, Bill had an inner experience so shattering that when he tried to explain what had happened he concluded by saying, "There are no words to describe it."

At the time, although he felt free and at peace, Bill thought he must be hallucinating, and he yelled for Dr. Silkworth.

The doctor came on the run and cross-examined Bill like a trial lawyer going after a criminal. He poked and probed at every aspect of what had happened to Bill, making him describe it in as many different ways as he could. Then he thought for a moment and said, "No, Bill, you are not crazy. I've read about such things. Sometimes spiritual experiences do release people from alcoholism."

Release was exactly what had come to Bill. He never took another drink. While still in the hospital, he began to plan a method of helping alcoholics by which one former drinker would sober up another, just as Ebby had helped him, until the disease was completely stamped out. He left the hospital, and he and Ebby started rounding up drunks, sharing their

78

experience and the Oxford Group guidelines, and trying to help them get off alcohol. The two friends failed miserably. They won no recruits, but at least they stayed sober.

As Bill stood in the Mayflower lobby staring at the church directory on the wall in front of him, he realized that he hadn't had a drink since last December. Yet he still wanted to get drunk right then and there, in Akron, Ohio, on the day before Mother's Day. For the first time in his life, Bill panicked at the thought of drinking, of getting drunk again. The panic saved his life as his thoughts cleared and he recalled how he had stayed sober for nearly half a year by trying to help other people. The realization slammed home: "You need another alcoholic to talk to! You need another alcoholic just as much as he needs you!" The white letters dancing on the bulletin board came into focus, telling him exactly where he could find one.

Bill picked a church name and phone number at random from the listing on the directory, went up to his room, and dialed the church. Walter Trunks, an Episcopal priest, came on the line. At first Father Trunks seemed to think Bill was a crackpot who had already had too much to drink, but the former drinker succeeded in making it clear that, in order to hang onto his own sobriety, he needed to talk with someone who had a drinking problem. Father Trunks said he thought he could help. He gave Bill a list of ten people who might be able to put him in touch with an alcoholic.

One after another, Bill telephoned the people on the hastily scribbled list. Nine of them were not

79

home. The tenth name, Mrs. Henrietta Seiberling, reminded Bill of another Seiberling he had met years earlier on Wall Street, the man who had founded Goodyear Rubber Company. Bill couldn't bring himself to call a woman who was probably the wife of a former business acquaintance and tell her his problem, and he left his room, went down to the lobby, and started pacing again. The clink of glasses grew louder, the chatter more animated. Bill knew he couldn't hold out much longer. He had to speak to another alcoholic, or he would drink. Finally, he returned to his room and called Mrs. Seiberling.

That call started a chain of events that revolutionized Bill's life. Mrs. Seiberling, who turned out to be a daughter-in-law of the man Bill had known, did put him in touch with another alcoholic, a surgeon named Dr. Bob S. He soon became, with Bill W., the cofounder of Alcoholics Anonymous, A.A., a fellowship that eventually numbered over 900,000 people who help each other to stay sober and who reach out to help those alcoholics who are still drinking. A.A. broke fairly quickly with the Oxford Groups, for effective as the groups were for some people, their tightly organized religious movement seemed to drive away more alcoholics than it helped. The basic Oxford guidelines, however, became A.A.'s own program of recovery. Today, they have been expanded into the Twelve Suggested Steps for Recovery which form the basis of sober living for hundreds of thousands of problem drinkers.

But all that was in the future. The key to the whole A.A. movement was the insight that had first gotten Bill sober in New York and had kept him sober that May evening in Akron: one alcoholic told his drinking story to another, reliving and sharing the experience of how his drinking had progressed from a pleasant social pastime to an uncontrollable compulsion that had made him powerless over alcohol.

"I just talked about my own case," Bill said later in describing his first meeting with Dr. Bob. "Our talk was a completely mutual thing. I knew that I needed this alcoholic as much as he needed me."

Bill told Dr. Bob about his boyhood in Vermont and explained how he had first started drinking in the army during World War I because he discovered that it was easier for him to make friends and communicate with people when he had some alcohol under his belt. He described how he had returned from the war, studied law, and gone to Wall Street dreaming of a swift rise to wealth and power through speculation in the stock market—dreams entirely fueled by alcohol.

He recalled the failures in his business career after the stock market crash of 1929, and he talked of how he had used alcohol to escape from disappointment. He explained how each effort to make a comeback became harder and harder as the years passed—and less and less successful. He relived for his new friend the early 1930s, when he and Lois had to move in with her family in Brooklyn, and how she went to work to support them both by clerking in a department store. He told how he had stolen from her purse the few dollars she brought home so that he could buy liquor, and he described the guilt and shame he felt because of what he was

81

doing. "I was drinking to numb the pain, to forget," he told Dr. Bob.

By coincidence, Dr. Bob was also from Vermont. He had barely scraped through medical school on account of his own bouts with the bottle, and his marriage and career were teetering on the brink of disaster. He sat for hours that first night, shaking his head in agreement and repeating, "Yes, that's me, I'm like that." Within a month, he, too, had his last drink, and he devoted the rest of his life to working with Bill to help free others crushed under the yoke of alcoholism.

In shared experience, a fellowship was formed between two alcoholics on a May night in Akron, Ohio. One man's shared hope became the hope of two, then of three, and over the years, of multitudes. Because Bill W. picked up a phone instead of a drink, he opened a way for men and women, oldsters and teen-agers, that could lead them to freedom from alcoholism. He showed them that they could put down their drinks and that they never had to pick them up again.

7.
Martin
de Porres

Lay Brother

Eleven-year-old Martin de Porres was finding out that some choices are harder to make than others. Here he was in Guayaquil, Ecuador, living in the fine house of his father's uncle, Don Diego de Miranda. In the recently conquered Spanish colonies, wealth and power could achieve great things, even for a half-breed son of a Spanish nobleman and a freed black woman. Martin had been told that he could stay with Don Diego, even though his own father, Don Juan de Porres, would be leaving to become governor of Panama. If Martin stayed in Guayaquil, Don Diego would see that the boy completed his medical studies and began a medical practice consisting of high-paying patients from the noble class.

Martin's other option was to return to Lima, Peru, to live with his mother, Ana Velasquez, and his sister. Three years earlier, Don Juan de Porres, a nobleman of Alcántara, Spain, had returned to Lima, sought out Ana Velasquez, and taken Martin, eight, and Juana, seven, to Guayaquil to be educated. He could not take their mother. It would not be proper for a Spanish knight to take a black woman to live with him, even though she was the mother of his children.

Martin had promised his mother that he would return, and now that his father was going to Panama, Martin felt that his duty was clear.

Don Juan and Don Diego argued long and hard with the boy. A half-breed, especially one who was half Black and half Spanish, they said, was on the bottom rung in Lima. Even the Indians, whose nation had been wiped out only fifty-five years earlier when Pizarro demolished the Inca Empire, looked down on half-breeds of Negro blood. In Guayaquil, they told Martin, he could finish his training, set up his medical practice, and become a man of standing and influence in the community. Don Diego would see to that. In Lima, he would be nothing, worse than nothing.

As he weighed their arguments, Martin thought back to the first years of his life. He and Juana had lived with their mother in a mud shack, sleeping on mats on the dirt floor. There was never enough to eat, and their clothes were little more than rags. Even though he was only eight when they had left Lima, he could remember how the Spanish and the Indians wanted no part of the two children whose mother was a black and whose father was unknown.

Now, his father and his granduncle were persuasive, and he longed to give in, to follow their advice, to take the easy road to wealth and power. After all, as a doctor he could help people, even in Guayaquil. All his patients need not be wealthy. He could serve the poor and God as well by healing the sick and needy right there in Ecuador. Why should he give up all that was being held out to him?

But for Martin, the answer was clear enough. His heart told him he belonged in Lima. His mother was there. His people, the poor and the sick of the city, were there. He believed that God wanted him there. So to Lima he went, as an apprentice to Dr. Marcelo de Rivero, thanks to his granduncle's influence. Juana stayed behind in Ecuador to be educated.

Dr. de Rivero was an outstanding physician and a kind man. He grew fond of Martin, who proved to be a capable student who possessed a real gift for healing. Slowly, the doctor's patients also came to like and accept the young half-breed, and everything went well until, after five years of study, Martin disappeared. He was no longer to be seen practicing his healing arts beside his wise tutor. He no longer went with Dr. de Rivero to visit the sick.

Martin de Porres had become convinced that God wanted him to make an even deeper commitment to service, and when he was fifteen, he went to the Convent of the Holy Rosary, a Dominican priory in Lima—as a servant. Martin had made another choice. Again, it was a choice that must have seemed foolish, perhaps even crazy, to those who knew him. First he gave up the chance to become important in Guayaquil. Then, when he was succeeding well as an apprentice physician, he threw over his chosen profession and went to sweep floors in a Dominican priory. In those first years with the Dominicans, Martin may have wondered why he made the choices he did. But being a person of deep faith, possessed of enough courage to follow his convictions even when they seemed to go against everything common sense told him, Martin probably had little doubt that God's call to join the Dominicans would somehow help him serve God's poor better than he could have served them as a doctor. So he swept floors, cut hair, mended the friars' robes, tended the garden, and cleaned the toilets. At the same time, he nursed the sick friars and any poor people who crossed his path.

Martin was doing all these things in a Dominican convent, yet he refused to become a Dominican friar himself. Not that he was discriminated against. His superiors urged him to take the vows and don the habit of a Dominican lay brother, but Martin refused. He chose the humblest life possible, without even the consolation of full membership in the order.

When Martin had been in the convent for four years, word reached his father in the Governor's Palace in Panama that his son was with the Dominicans. But the news that fell on Don Juan's ears was upsetting. The lad had refused to become a full-fledged Dominican. Don Juan de Porres wrote to the superior of the convent and told him that Martin, son of a Spanish nobleman, must be given the vows of the order and consecrated a priest. The superior had no objection, and he confronted Martin.

When his father's wishes were put to him, Martin broke into tears and begged to be allowed to remain exactly as he was. The superior had never seen him so upset. Martin was usually a calm, obedient young man. However, on this matter, he proved to be as bullheaded as any teen-ager could be. His calling, he said, was humble service—no vows, no priesthood. If God wanted otherwise, he would make his will known and show Martin how to carry it out. Reluctantly, for one did not casually go against the wishes of an important Spanish nobleman, the superior let the matter drop, and Martin happily went back to his floors and his latrines.

Young as he was, the half-breed brother began to acquire a reputation for more than average devotion to his religion and to the rules of the order. Discipline could grow lax in the far corners of the Spanish Empire. Saint Dominic's rule might prescribe that his monks wear a strict tonsure—a head completely shaved except for a slight ring of hair around the sides—but far from the strict practices that prevailed in European priories, vanity could creep in.

Father Santiago was one friar who thought he was special. He kept a few curls in the front part of his tonsure. It made him look more fashionable. One day, Martin cut Father Santiago's hair without being aware of the priest's special tastes. He followed the rule book, snipping off the curls along with every other strand of hair that didn't belong in a Dominican's tonsure.

When the priest saw what the young brother had done, he was furious. Who was this mere boy to tell him how Saint Dominic wanted him to wear his hair? He let Martin know exactly how he felt, and he warned him to watch his step the next time. Martin was caught—he could not disobey the rule, yet Father Santiago obviously outranked him. Fortunately, hair grows slowly, and some superiors, at least, are able to catch a hint, even one suggested by the conduct of a simple brother, that discipline may have grown lax. Before Father Santiago had time to raise another crop of curls, word came from the prior that everyone—no exceptions—was to wear the regulation tonsure. By doing the right thing as he was given to see it, Brother Martin was helping others to see the right thing to do.

Discipline may have become a little slack in the Convent of the Holy Rosary in Lima, but it was not because the Dominican friars were overly rich. The priory was so poor that one day the superior decided to sell a valuable painting to help pay the convent's debts. He took the picture off the wall and headed out the door in search of a buyer. When Martin learned that the prior had been reduced to selling the treasures of the community, he took off and caught up with his superior before he was able to make a sale.

"Don't sell the painting, Father Prior," he pleaded. "Look at me. I'm young and strong. I'll sell myself to someone as a servant until I earn enough to pay our debts." Martin probably made that offer on the spur of the moment. Very little time could have passed between the moment he learned of the superior's decision and the moment when he finally caught up with him. Yet it was from the heart, a sincere reflection of Martin's devotion to the priory and its needs.

Stunned, the father superior made a different decision. He told Martin that he could no longer refuse to take the vows of the Dominican order. He could continue to refuse to be ordained a priest, although he was certainly worthy and intelligent enough to be ordained; however, he must become a full-blown Dominican, as totally and permanently a member of the order as any other priest or lay brother in the Convent of the Holy Rosary. He put the matter beyond debate by telling Martin that it was a command.

Convinced that God had spoken through the mouth of father prior, Martin de Porres returned to the convent and prepared to enter officially the family of Saint Dominic. In 1603, at the age of twenty-four, he prostrated himself before the altar in the convent's chapel, swore his vows, and donned the black and white robes of a Dominican lay brother.

Years passed. Stories multiplied about strange and wonderful things done by the quiet and gentle lay brother. People said he talked to animals and birds. They said he worked marvels on the sick, although Brother Martin himself claimed that whatever he accomplished was because of the herbal medicines he used and the goodness of God. Brother Martin became an active friend of the poor. He planted fig and olive groves on unowned land that he claimed in the name of the city's needy, and he filled the convent's cells with the sick and homeless until he was explicitly forbidden by his superior to do so.

One day when Brother Martin was out helping the poor people, he was so busy that he hadn't noticed how dark it was getting. Afraid he would be late, he rushed home, almost stumbling over a figure propped against the walls of the priory. He stopped and spoke to the figure, an old man who made no reply. Brother Martin stooped and tried to get a better look, and what met his eyes was not pleasant. The old beggar was filthy, covered with bloody, pus-infected sores. His eyes were closed. Martin felt for the man's heartbeat and could scarcely detect it. Regardless of the prior's command, Brother Martin hoisted the fragile body onto his shoulders and crept quietly into the convent to his cell. He tended the old man's sores, brought him food, and slept on the floor while the old man rested on his bed. After a few days, the beggar was strong enough to leave the convent, just as stealthily as he had arrived.

Martin sneaked him out and returned to his cell to find that he had been caught red-handed. Another lay brother stared in disgust at the blood-stained bedding on Martin's cot. The brother went straight to the prior and told him that Brother Martin had disobeyed orders, brought another sick person into the convent, and even put the wretched creature in his own bed and ruined good sheets and blankets!

The prior summoned Martin. "You have done wrong, brother," he said. "You have disobeyed a superior's order. Do you understand what you have done?"

Martin looked at the man to whom he had surrendered control over his life through the vow of obedience. "I'm not sure I do understand, father superior," he said. "Can it truly be wrong to put charity before obedience?"

The superior had no answer. Perhaps, he was

thinking to himself, those who have the simplicity of saints can be complicated people to live with.

Martin de Porres did amazing things all his life, and he managed to get himself into hot water more than once. In his time, as is still common today in many countries, to be married, a young woman had to have a dowry, a certain amount of money to bring to her husband. Martin's sister, Juana, came at last back to Lima, well educated and ready to be married to a fine husband. She asked Martin to hold her dowry, a bagful of gold pieces, until her wedding day. Martin took the bag and hid it in his cell. Then, as usual, he met some poor people, and that was the end of the dowry. He gave it to them to buy food and clothing. When he realized what he had done, even Martin was worried. He had no right to give away his sister's dowry—even to the poor. She would be disgraced on her wedding day. Perhaps the wedding would be canceled.

He decided to trust in God to replace the gold. After all, they were God's poor. On the day before the wedding, Martin went to visit a couple he knew. He told the husband, Don Mateo Pastor, what had happened. Don Mateo, who was a chemist, scolded Martin for acting so carelessly with Juana's money. He told Martin that some of the people weren't even really poor; they were just taking advantage of his kindness. Perhaps they were the ones who had gotten Juana's dowry.

"Isn't it better to be taken advantage of ten times than to neglect one needy human being even once?" Martin asked him.

The chemist had no answer, and when he told his

wife what Brother Martin had done, she also scolded Martin. Sadly, Martin went back to the convent. The next day, Don Mateo and his wife appeared at the church where Juana was being married, and just before the ceremony, they handed Martin de Porres a little leather pouch that contained the amount of gold needed for Juana's dowry. They had paid it from their own savings.

Most people would simply be grateful to have been saved, even at the last minute, from the consequences of being generous with someone else's money. Not Martin. He decided that the kind of generosity the Pastors had shown should be spread around. After all, there were many girls in Lima who came from families so poor that there was no money for dowries. As a result, they could not be married or become nuns. They were forced to be servants or beggars. Martin explained his idea to the Pastors, who were good enough and generous enough to see the truth in what Brother Martin said. They promised to find the money to make up dowries for twenty-seven young women. Martin thought that was so fine that he went about Lima telling the rich Spaniards how they could do the same. He was quiet in his pleading, but he was also forceful, and soon there was a permanent dowry fund for poor girls. Martin arranged for the dowry to come as a gift from the community, for he did not want the girls to be embarrassed by feeling that they were accepting charity.

Martin opened a school, the Orphanage and School of the Holy Cross, where paid teachers trained poor young men and women in trades that would enable them to earn a decent living. In his mother's house, he started a free clinic for the sick. He even pawned his hat one day to buy a loaf of bread for some poor prisoners because he had no money when they asked him for food.

In the twentieth century, we have large institutions with professional staffs to take care of the kind of needs Martin de Porres tried to meet with his own wit and his love of neighbor. We would consider someone like him, for the most part, slightly daft—kind, to be sure, but a little off-center in his approach to reality—an oddball.

A great many people in Lima started out describing Martin de Porres in precisely those terms. After all, he kept going outside the established channels and violating the usual order of things. He was unsophisticated enough to think that a religious order's rule meant exactly what it said and that it ought to be obeyed. He was simpleminded enough to think that charity might sometimes come before obedience. He was so liberal minded about the idea of attending to the needs of the poor that he thought they might need the convent's beds more than the religious who already occupied them.

People in Lima may have begun by considering Martin de Porres a crackpot, but they soon realized he was a saint. When he went to God, on November 3, 1639, everyone in Peru—from the king's viceroy to the poorest half-breed—knew that they had lost not just a religious brother, but a brother.

8.
Vincent
Capodanno
Chaplain

To many people, Lieutenant Vincent R. Capodanno might have seemed the wrong man in the wrong place at the wrong time. A priest, he lived among cursing, killing marines. A missionary ordained to spread the good news of "Peace on earth, good will to all men," he spent the last eighteen months of his life in the midst of violence and death. Vincent Capodanno died in a war few understood and most didn't want. And he volunteered for the assignment.

By 1967, when Capodanno arrived in Vietnam, the United States was beginning to suffer internal strife over that seemingly futile conflict in a small, almost unknown Asian nation. To the people in the peace movement, called *doves,* the U.S. was engaged in a military action that violated the principles upon which this nation had been founded. In Ho Chi Minh, leader of the North Vietnamese, the doves saw a true freedom fighter, a present-day George Washington, leading an oppressed people in their struggle to be free.

The Chinese, the Japanese, and the French had kept Vietnam's people under the control of foreign occupation. When France withdrew when the cost of remaining became too high, the United States moved in to fill the vacuum. A handful of U.S. "military advisers" swelled to hundreds of thousands of troops as millions of dollars and countless tons of explosives were poured into Southeast Asia in an attempt to prop up one corrupt regime after another to keep South Vietnam from going Communist. The doves accused their country of seeking to annihilate a tiny nation of absolutely no strategic importance solely to keep the Communists out of power. The doves delighted in quoting one general who was reported in the national press to have said, "We had to destroy the village to save it." It was as if John Wayne had been exposed as a wifebeater and child abuser. We ought to have known better, the doves said. We ought to be ashamed of ourselves.

On the other hand, there were people, called *hawks*, who saw Vietnam, not through the rose-colored glasses of idealism, but through the stark red prism of cold war logic. Ho Chi Minh was a Communist. Communism, in the wake of World War II, had spread from Russia throughout Eastern Europe, to China, North Korea, Cuba, and, finally, Vietnam. Behind slight nationalistic differences, the Communist bloc, the hawks said, was just that—a bloc, a group of nations dominated by a common political vision. Hadn't kindly "Uncle Nikita" Khrushchev boasted, "We shall bury you!"?

Vietnam, declared the hawks, was where the Western world had to draw the line and hold it. If

Vietnam went Communist, they argued, the rest of Southeast Asia, like a bunch of stacked dominoes, would soon topple. "Here you stop," had to be the message of Vietnam, and the point had to be driven home by all the weaponry the world's strongest economy could produce.

So Vietnamese peasants, and American and oriental soldiers poured their blood on the rich soil of Vietnam, and the United States bled internally from an inner wrenching the nation had not known since the Civil War a century earlier. And as in the Civil War, Vietnam pitted brother against brother and father against son.

A young man would proudly put on the uniform of his country, as his father and grandfather had done before him in a patriotic tradition of citizen soldiers stretching back two centuries. He would march off to fight—perhaps to die—in a part of the world he had never heard of for a cause he didn't really know or care about. He went because his nation had called him to arms, just as the farmer-patriots had done when they faced British musket fire on the bridge at Concord in the dim mists of the Revolutionary War.

While one son went dutifully to Vietnam, his brother fled in anguish and shame to Canada or Sweden, not out of cowardice or fear, but because he was convinced that his country was involved in an unjust war, that he would be forced to kill innocent people with deadly weapons in a land where he had no business being. Vietnam, claimed the draft resister, had the same right to self-determination as the United States had claimed in 1776. The U.S. had no business interfering in another nation's internal politics. To kill in such a cause, no matter what America's leaders claimed, was unjustifiable and immoral, large-scale murder. To resist such a war—even if it meant exile from one's homeland—was a courageous act, a choice of good over evil, of life over death.

In the spring of 1965, to such a war, in such a divided time, came Vincent Capodanno, a man consecrated to things of the spirit, set down by his own decision amid the most efficient combat troops his nation could field.

Capodanno did not set out to be a marine chaplain. His original choice was a life of service in foreign lands as a Maryknoll missioner. In making this choice, he was seeking to resolve a contradiction that had plagued humankind from the beginning. He was seeking to sow love where there was hatred; pardon where there was injury; life where there was death.

Choosing to share the mud and heat of Vietnam with a group of men whose mission was death and whose gospel was kill or be killed was an outgrowth of his earlier decision, perhaps a harsher way of testing the sincerity of his motives. Whatever his reasons, Vincent Capodanno sealed his mission with his own blood.

Throughout the ages, men have gone to war for many reasons: glory, wealth, power, self-defense, or even because it was fashionable to gallop a white charger into the cannon's roaring mouth. Capodanno went to war for the same reason he had gone as a missionary to Taiwan. Vietnam was a place God seemed to have forsaken. Someone had to say that no place is ever abandoned by divine love, and that was Capodanno's mission in Maryknoll. That was his mission as a marine.

At some point during his years at Curtis High School in Staten Island, New York, young Vinnie chose his mission when he decided to join the ranks of those who leave father and mother, sister and brother, to serve their God by serving the least of his children. He entered Maryknoll, the Catholic Foreign Mission Society of America, as the most likely group to help him achieve that goal.

Young Capodanno probably learned about Vietnam long before most Americans even knew it existed. One of Maryknoll's houses of study, the Venard, just outside Scranton, Pennsylvania, had been named for a French missionary, Blessed Theophane Venard, a priest who had been killed in Annam, North Vietnam, during the nineteenth century. Bishop James A. Walsh, one of Maryknoll's cofounders, had translated into English a biography of the French missionary, and it was commonly assigned as inspirational reading for seminarians. The Vietnam described in the saint's life was probably little more than a place-name to Capodanno and his fellow students, an obscure country in a forgotten corner of the globe. It couldn't have been too important, for Maryknoll didn't even have missioners there.

The Vietnam that screamed from the headlines during the mid-1960s was an entirely different world. American troops passing through Taiwan spoke of that Vietnam. The horror of the experience, written in the hollow eyes and gaunt faces of those men, held an unspoken reproach for Capodanno: here on lovely Taiwan you serve as parish priest to a colorful group of natives. Their costumes and dances are a tourist attraction. All is happiness and gaiety. It must be delightful to preach a Gospel of love and forgiveness in such a place. What of us, those whom God has forgotten? We kill, and our countrymen call us butchers. We die because old women and children plant mines that blow our feet and legs off. Is your Gospel for us? Does your God want to know us? Who will come and speak your God's name in the blood and muck where we pitch our tents?

The challenge may never have been spoken, but it was there in the eyes of every soldier Capodanno met. His answer was to request permission to enter training as a military chaplain. Permission given, he attended the U.S. Naval Chaplains School at Newport, Rhode Island, and was commissioned a lieutenant, Chaplain Corps, U.S. Naval Reserve, on December 28, 1965. Volunteering for a chalplain's berth wasn't enough. Capodanno volunteered for duty in Vietnam, and that request was granted, too.

In 1966, he joined the first Marines in Da Nang. From then on, his parishioners were the "grunts"— the marine rifle platoons. Where they went, Chaplain Capodanno went too. When the tropical sun beat down on the troopers, he dripped with sweat and licked his parched lips. When the rains fell in a solid wall of water, he stumbled through knee-deep mud and huddled in a molding sleeping bag looking for rest that would not come.

There is a photograph of Vincent Capodanno

conducting a religious service for his marines. He is thirty-seven, yet his crew-cut hair is gray. Rumpled fatigues hang shapelessly on a lanky torso. His face is the face of a man who has lived too close to death for too long. No vestments, no altar or candles appear in the photo, just a book of ritual in the priest's hand. A few marines sit before him on the grass. His backdrop is the lush jungle. Religion, like everything else in war-ridden Vietnam, had been stripped of frills. But what counted was there because Vincent Capodanno was there. The first Marines, somewhere south of Da Nang, sent to search and destroy, to kill and to die, knew that God had not abandoned them.

One day, as he knew it must, death claimed the thirty-seven-year-old chaplain at an obscure outpost in Queson Valley. On September 4, in the midst of an assault against North Vietnamese regulars, Lieutenant Capodanno was in the company command post enjoying what little rest and security its sandbag walls and roof could provide. Word came that the Second Platoon of M Company was in danger of being overrun by an enemy assault. Without a moment's hesitation, Capodanno raced from the headquarters bunker and zigzagged his way across open ground as machine gun bullets raised puffs of dirt all around him. He had one goal—to be with the platoon that was under attack. That's where he was needed, and that's where he was headed.

Automatic weapons chattered in staccato. Cannons arched their lethal cargo of explosives. Capodanno, preoccupied with the needs of the wounded and dying marines, calmly crawled through the dirt, touching shattered bodies, comforting and offering forgiveness to men who had already been chewed up and spat out by the battle. As the dying men prepared to meet their God, Capodanno offered what comfort he could to those who had little left to ask and no one else to ask it of.

Suddenly the chaplain felt himself hurled into the air and smashed in a heap on the ground. Dazed, torn by pain, he realized that a mortar round had hit near him; shrapnel riddled his arms and legs, and part of his right hand had been blown off. A marine medic spotted the wounded chaplain and moved toward him, but the priest waved the corpsman off, yelling to him to take care of the wounded troopers. Meanwhile, Capodanno started crawling toward the dead and dying, his movements slowed by pain and loss of blood. His men needed him. In this hell of pain and death, his was the only voice of hope, of comfort. He must not be stilled. He must ease the last minutes of his fallen comrades. He must keep going, no matter the agony of his wounds.

Capodanno spotted a young wounded medic sprawled on the ground ahead of him. Less than fifty feet away, a Vietnamese machine gunner was taking aim. With no thought for his own safety, Capodanno struggled to reach the medic and pull him out of the line of fire. He stumbled through his own pain to save the corpsman, and when he had but inches to go, round after round slammed into the priest's body. The machine gun had been turned on him. A stream of bullets tore the life from his body, and Vincent Capodanno fell dead, another American watering with his blood the red soil of Vietnam.

Nations give medals to brave men, and the United States gave a medal to Lieutenant Vincent R. Capodanno. The president of the United States, in the name of Congress, bestowed on him the Medal of Honor, the highest military award the nation can give in recognition of an act of heroism. The Honorable Paul R. Ignatius, secretary of the navy, presented the medal to Lieutenant Capodanno's brother James at the Washington Navy Yard at 1030 hours (10:30 in the morning) on January 7, 1969, some four months after the priest was cut down.

Months and years passed. America continued to be split into two increasingly hostile camps. The navy commissioned a frigate, *FF 1093*, the U.S.S. *Capodanno*, and the official press release boasted that she had a homing torpedo launching system, twin mounted torpedo tubes, a 5″/54 rapid-fire gun, and even a SH-2F LAMPS helicopter. Meanwhile, the Vietnam Veterans Against the War, many in wheelchairs or on crutches, besieged the White House and threw their combat medals over the wrought iron fence surrounding the official home of our nation's first family.

Staten Island rechristened Seaside Boulevard naming it Father Capodanno Boulevard in honor of its fallen native son.

The National Marine Corps Scholarship Foundation set up a fund in Lieutenant Capodanno's honor. And draft-age young men fled American campuses in growing numbers to avoid being drafted to fight in the war that had killed him.

Lieutenant Vincent Capodanno, Father Vincent

Capodanno, lay in his grave, torn apart by bullets in a war he did not fight but chose to endure. In him, the contradictions of that military action and of his nation come to a head. The hawks could lay a medal on his tomb. The doves could see in his fearless commitment to those who needed him the ultimate witness that love does conquer hate, peace does overcome violence.

"What an example," said navy doctor Joseph LaHood about Capodanno. "He served; he indicated without words that Christ was there. They, the marines, will never forget that he was one of them, this priest of God, this hero."

"Wherever the marines are, Father C. is there," recalled a marine lieutenant named Ryan. "In the water or in mud up to his knees. He was the greatest man I ever knew. He went where we went, and his only weapon was faith."

9.
Francis Xavier
Ford

Bishop

*Grant us, Lord, to be the doorstep by which the
multitudes may come to worship Thee. And if, in
the saving of their souls, we are ground underfoot and spat upon and worn out, at least we
shall have served Thee in some small way in
helping pagan souls; we shall have become the
King's Highway in pathless China.*

—Bishop Francis X. Ford

There is an old Arabian proverb that says, "Be
careful of what you pray for, because you may get
it," although Frank Ford had probably never heard
it when he composed his prayer on the day he was
consecrated a bishop for service in Kaying, China, in
1935. Had he heard it, the forty-three-year-old missioner most likely would have gone ahead and composed his prayer anyway. Francis Xavier Ford meant
every word he was saying in that prayer, and when
the time came to back those words with action, he
was not found wanting.

Bishop Ford's prayer seems quaint today, with its

talk of pagans and saving souls. Language, like clothing, goes in and out of fashion, and nobody uses words like those today. If Frank Ford were writing his prayer now, his choice of words might be different, but his goal would remain the same: to bring God to people and people to God. And he would still be willing to go the whole distance, even to the point of giving up his life if necessary. Frank Ford didn't do things by half measures, and he didn't drag his feet once he had made a commitment.

In 1912, Frank decided to become a Maryknoll missioner after hearing a talk by the new organization's cofounder, Father James A. Walsh. Frank was a senior at Cathedral High School in New York City, preparing to be a priest in his home diocese of Brooklyn, when the priest from Boston told of his plan to supply young American men and women to lands overseas where the Church was either nonexistent or in a state of near collapse.

Maybe Frank Ford thought of the saint in whose name he had been christened, Francis Xavier, the great Jesuit missionary to the Orient. Maybe he simply felt the tug of adventure. Whatever the reason, Father Walsh's words fell on open ears and a willing heart. He had scarcely finished his talk to the students when a small, wiry teen-ager approached him. Young Frank Ford said he wanted to join Maryknoll, and thus he became the first student recruited for the new venture.

Frank would chalk up a string of firsts before he was through. He would be among the first priests ordained into the Catholic Foreign Mission Society of America, popularly known as Maryknoll. He would be in the first group of four men sent to serve in China. He would be the first American missionary consecrated a bishop. He would be the first bishop to send women out into the villages and hamlets of the rural China to live and work with the people. And he would be the first American missionary to shed his blood as the red tide of communism swept over his adopted land.

The heroic ending of Frank Ford's life was worthy of its beginning. At the height of the potato famine in 1846, his grandparents had left Ireland, sailing with three sons and a daughter from Galway Bay to Boston. Eamon Ford, the patriarch of the clan, found work as a printer, and at the age of sixty enlisted in the Union army along with his two sons, Austin and Patrick, serving throughout the Civil War in the Ninth Massachusetts Regiment. A third son, Thomas, had already joined the Union navy, and he made the supreme sacrifice for his homeland when his ship, the U.S.S. *Cumberland*, was sent to the bottom by the Confederate ironclad *Merrimac*.

Five years after the war ended, Frank's father, Austin, and his uncle, Patrick, founded the newspaper, *Irish World*, a rallying point for the hundreds of thousands of people who had left Ireland's poverty, famine, and religious persecution to seek a better life in the United States. The *Irish World* became the first paper in the U.S. to reach a circulation of one million, and Austin Ford's militant support of Irish independence became such a powerful voice that it was declared a penal offense in Great Britain and Ireland to have a copy of the paper in one's possession.

The *Irish World* gave its editor a far-reaching public forum, and it gave him a wife as well. Elizabeth Rellihan Ford was a farm girl in Iowa when she started submitting articles to the *Irish World*. Six years after the paper's founding, she was invited by Austin Ford to come to New York to join its editorial staff, and within a year, she had added to her duties as staff writer the roles of wife and mother.

Sixth in a family of four boys and four girls, Francis Xavier was born prematurely on January 11, 1892. For four weeks, his mother had to wrap the frail infant in flannel cloths soaked in olive oil, hoping that he could absorb enough nourishment through his skin to keep him alive.

As Frank Ford was growing up, such leading figures of the day trooped through his parents' house as political leaders Michael Davitt, Charles Stewart Parnell, and John Redmond; Terence Powderly and Samuel Gompers, who were pioneers in the labor union movement; and Victor Herbert, the composer.

One day, Frank's father showed him a picture of his namesake, Saint Francis Xavier. "There's a man for you, Francis. Be like him," Austin Ford said to his young son, and he would live to see his son take those words literally.

Frank wrote of another early influence in his decision to become a missioner. He had heard an "old China hand" give a talk in his parish church in Brooklyn.

"He was a Father Conrardy, a fiery enthusiast, and his subject was his lifework among the lepers," Ford wrote. "He gloried in his love for them and flung the challenge in our face to show our Catholicity by helping him to build a home for them. It seemed harder for him to beg for money than to do the disgusting work of nursing slowly rotting Chinese men and women, but he traveled Europe and America for funds. With a generous impulse I put a nickel in the basket, five times my usual sum, and the rest of the mass was spent in repeating to myself Father Conrardy's last words: 'My one ambeesch is to die a martyr!' "

Frank Ford may not have said publicly that he had the "ambeesch"—the ambition—"to die a martyr." But he could not rule out that possibility as Mao Tse-tung's Red Army battled its way through China in the late 1940s. He didn't flinch from the prospect that staying at his post might cost him his life, and as head of the Kaying Diocese, he started preparing those working under him for it as well.

In 1949, shortly before Kaying was occupied by the Red Army, he wrote: "Pain and suffering may be God's plan to purify our motives. Pain accepted in advance may be God's way to unite us more clearly to Himself. . . . You must not expect Heaven on earth. As Christians we should share the Cross. Perhaps suffering is the only way we can expiate the sins of the world, our own and others. This should not worry or terrify us. 'I can do all things in Him who strengtheneth me.' "

Although the fast-moving little bishop didn't rule out the possibility of death, he refused to sit glumly by and wait for it. He continued working on the cathedral he had started after the war. It was his commitment to the future, a pledge of hope from a man who had written, "Hope at all times, and not merely in a crisis; this is the essential missionary virtue." And he kept his sense of humor. It comes through in the bishop's description of himself (the pastor) and his parishioners as they moved the church furnishings from the private house he had been using as a church into the newly finished basement of the cathedral, the only part of the structure he could afford to finish:

"Vested in cope and towering like Saint Boniface before the druids' oak, the pastor sprinkled holy water on each group as the different sodalists came, two by two, burdened with a pew between them. He even improvised a 'Procedamus in Pace' (Let us proceed in peace), the signal for the procession.

"The old men and women were given the lighted candles from the altar, the missal and altar cards, the Stations of the Cross, and holy water stoups to carry. The carpets were lifted in their dusty clouds of glory, and the sanctuary rail was taken in sections. The younger men and women raised their pews and, led by the crossbearer and acolytes, in somewhat unliturgical processional moved through the fields and streets. At a decent interval, the pastor followed with the Blessed Sacrament, and then a new life began for the parish."

Frank Ford would soon need that sense of humor and that steadfast hope. He was aware of the approaching collapse of Chiang Kai-shek's regime and the inevitable Communist take-over that would follow.

"No matter how dark the world around us," he reminded those with him in Kaying, "how huge the task ahead of us, the thought that 'God is good' can send us smiling through life." That was not wishful thinking on the part of an ivory-tower cleric. It was the deliberate conclusion reached by a highly intelligent man who knew that he would probably be looking down a Communist gun barrel in the near future.

In 1950, as Mao's victorious troops routed the last of Chiang's battered forces from the mainland of China, the Bamboo Curtain slammed shut. The persecution Bishop Ford had foreseen was not long in coming. The first warning came on December 12, when several of the bishop's priests and nuns were thrown into jail. In the days that followed, the thought of fleeing never seemed to have entered Ford's mind. He probably would have told anyone who suggested it what he had said to the U.S. consul who had warned him to leave China on the eve of World War II: "To leave is unthinkable. We must remain with our people."

His people felt the same way about their American pastor. Kaying, renamed Meihsien in the late 1940s, had known Christianity for almost three generations. There were many thousands of Christians, a strong Chinese clergy, and a widespread awareness on the part of the people that Bishop Francis Xavier Ford had given more than forty years of his life to China, most of it in Kaying, and had asked nothing in return. Kaying's Hakka people knew that the American had stayed at his post and endured Japanese bombing raids. He had shared their crude bomb shelters with them. As the Communist harassment of Christians stepped up its pace, the churches in Bishop Ford's diocese became more crowded than ever.

When he and his secretary, Sister Joan Marie, were finally arrested on December 23, 1950, the people sent a delegation to the local Red Army commander, telling him that he had made a mistake in arresting the bishop. The Red Army had indeed made a mistake, but not the kind the Christians of Meihsien had in mind.

The goal of the Communists had obviously been to publicly discredit and expel one of the most famous foreign churchmen in the area. In choosing Bishop Ford, they had overestimated their power and underestimated the loyalty of the local people. A decision was made to move Bishop Ford and Sister Joan Marie to Canton, where the bishop was not known and where a rigged trial could be more easily orchestrated. On April 14, 1951, the bishop and the nun were lined up in the courtyard of the bishop's house. Surrounded by thirty soldiers in full battle dress, the sixty-year-old bishop and his secretary, strained and haggard from more than four months of constant interrogation, stood silently with their arms tightly bound behind them and rope halters tied to their necks. Under the prodding of their guards, they shuffled down the streets of Meihsien to the bus depot, where they were put on a bus for Canton.

Hingning was the first stop. There the two Americans were stripped and beaten. "Not once did he try to defend himself," recalled Sister Joan Marie. They were marched through lines of Communist-led high school students who were armed with sticks, stones, and human refuse. Cries of "Death to the traitors! Death to the American spies!" accompanied their slow, painful progress. A student poked a stick between the bishop's legs and tripped him, and this act of pointless cruelty provoked howls of laughter from the other students. At one point, the crowd became so hate-crazed that they started beating the soldiers, too, and the panic-stricken guards fled, leaving the two prisoners at the mercy of the mob. Finally, the two missionaries were rescued and placed in separate jail cells, and people paraded by their cells throughout the night shouting insults. "Where is your God now?" they asked the prisoners. "What is he doing to help you?"

In the morning, the procession of pain was repeated. At Watchow, their next stop, Bishop Ford and his secretary were bound with heavier ropes that had been soaked in water so that they would bind more tightly after they had dried. The guards tied one rope so that it hung down the back of Bishop Ford's padded clerical gown, making him look like a monkey, an animal considered highly comical by the Chinese. Another stop brought more physical and verbal abuse, and finally, the duo arrived at the gate of Canton's main prison. A brief lull gave the bishop an opportunity to move close to the nun and whisper to her. His words, the last ever heard by a sympathetic listener, were etched into Sister Joan Marie's brain: "We're going to prison in honor of Christ, and it is no disgrace."

What Francis X. Ford endured over the next eighteen months will probably never be known.

Those who win revolutions seldom bother to record, much less release, the case histories of those who are ground up in the process of destroying the old to make way for the new. Enough missionaries, Protestant and Catholic, men and women, did survive to make it possible to reconstruct a grisly portrait of physical torture, nights of enforced sleeplessness, hunger, brainwashing, solitary confinement, and constant verbal abuse. Evidently the bishop did not break under the relentless attack of his captors. If he had, they would have used his surrender in their propaganda mills. Ultimately, his frail body could take no more pain and deprivation. As he had unwittingly prophesied in his prayer, Frank Ford died, "ground underfoot, spat upon and worn out."

Sister Joan Marie saw him three times, from a distance, before his death. The first time, he was being hurried along by another prisoner, probably back to his cell. The bishop stumbled and fell. The other prisoner, evidently a trustee, picked him up and slung him over his back. "I didn't see his face," Sister Joan Marie reported. "His legs hung limp like a rag doll. He was painfully thin." She remembered that the trustee and the guards had laughed at how ridiculous the old foreigner looked being toted along.

Two days later, toward the end of January 1952, the nun saw Bishop Ford again. "He was walking with great difficulty," she said, "taking very small steps. I got a good view of his face. He was emaciated and weak, and he looked like an old man of a hundred years. He had a beard that looked like white cotton. His hair was long and white. . . . I had the fleeting impression that his face was peaceful."

The last time the bishop's former secretary saw him, she caught only a glimpse. He was flung over another prisoner's shoulders like a lifeless sack.

Seven months passed. The nun, greatly weakened from her own ordeal, was called into the warden's office. She was shown photographs of Bishop Ford in bed, probably in a hospital. His face was gaunt, his eyes sunken. She could not even be certain, she said, whether the man in the photos was alive or dead. Her captors told her that the bishop had died on February 21, in spite of receiving the very best medical care. The cause of death, they said, was illness and old age. Several weeks later, Sister Joan Marie was brought to a run-down public cemetery in the countryside outside Canton. Her captors pointed to a stone marker on which was scrawled in still-fresh red paint, "Grave of Ford, February 21, 1952."

"We are in China to present a Gospel," Bishop Francis Xavier Ford had once told the priests and nuns of his diocese. "We are not schoolteachers, or medical doctors, or philanthropists." Deprived of human contact, of his sacred vessels and his church buildings, Frank Ford had preached that Gospel with the only thing left to him, his life. In so doing, he passed the test laid down two thousand years earlier by the risen Lord: "A man can have no greater love than to lay down his life for his friends."

10.
Abraham
Father of the
Faithful

The old man leaned against the gnarled trunk of the oak tree beneath which he and his three visitors had taken shelter from the hot sun. His thick body shook with laughter. Tears rolled down the leathery skin of his cheeks and disappeared into the white forest of his beard.

"I swear it to you, my lords," he said between fits of laughter, "that's what was told to me, and that's the promise I await."

The three handsome strangers sat on the rich carpets their host had spread on the ground for their comfort. Wrapped in costly garments, daggers of bronze with jewel-crested handles tucked into their waistbands, these travelers were obviously men of means, used to being treated with respect and given generous hospitality. They made no effort to join in their host's laughter.

Abraham, for that was the old man's name, scratched his head. He wondered why they failed to see the humor in the story he had shared with them. They could see he was an old man, long beyond the ability to father anyone, much less a people who would be as plentiful as the stars in the sky or the sands on the seashore. Surely they could see the absurdity of motherhood coming to Sarah, who stood beyond the tent baking bread for their supper. Stooped with age and dried as the desert sands under the midday sun, Sarah could no more conceive a child than she could fly—even if he were capable of fathering one.

"My lords, you fail to see the humor in my tale," the old chieftain said, passing a goatskin wine flask to his guests.

The three young men remained silent until each had drunk his fill of the wine. Then the middle one, the handsomest and most richly dressed, smiled gently and spoke, his voice melodious as the evening breeze of the desert.

"Abraham, son of Thare," he said, "it is not for us to believe or doubt you. You are a great desert chieftain, a man with many head of cattle and large herds of goats. The tents of your tribesmen and slaves stretch as far as the eye can see, almost to the horizon. Indeed, you are the father of many peoples, blessed with an army of kinsmen and gifted by the High One with great wealth. May not that be the message of the promise you speak of? Has not your god already kept his word? We do not laugh because we see all around us the evidence of a promise kept. Perhaps you have misunderstood your god. Did he not mean he would give you the multitude of kinfolk, the wealth and power you now possess? If you are lacking in gratitude to such a powerful god, surely you will feel his wrath for your hardness of heart."

118

"Noble lords," answered the desert chieftain, shaking his head so vehemently that his head covering almost fell off, "it is you who misunderstand me, not I who misunderstand my god, Yahweh. I am sorry if I appear to lack either gratitude or faith. Believe me, I lack neither. I do not even doubt that, if Yahweh says he will make a father out of an old goat like me and bring a child from the barren womb of Sarah, so shall he do. I do not doubt that he is a powerful and generous god. However, as a man of some intelligence and more than a little experience, I do reserve the right to consider the whole affair ridiculous. But then, I guess my life, and the life of my father, Thare, may his memory be blessed, has always seemed ridiculous to most people."

A faraway look came over the old man's face, and he settled himself more solidly against the tree trunk, propping up his heavy frame with ornamented pillows. He took a deep drink from the wineskin, as if preparing for a dry journey to a distant place.

His three listeners also passed the wine among themselves and settled down to listen to their host's narrative. In the desert, where the noise and distraction of the cities did not eat into a man's time and attention, there was always the luxury of many hours to appreciate a fine tale well told.

"I have repeated for you, my lords, the bare promise of Yahweh, given to me less than a year ago.

" 'I will make you most fruitful.' he told me. 'I will make you into nations, and your issue shall be kings.'

"Ridiculous as it may seem, my god has said he will produce rulers and great peoples from a wasted old fig like me and an ancient prune like Sarah. And that is not the first such promise. No, for that, you must go back to my father, Thare, son of Nahor.

"Thare was a great chieftain in his own right, and for many years we lived in the neighborhood of the city of Ur in the land of the Chaldeans."

Abraham's eyes glistened with the memory of past delights as he recalled the wealthy princes and beautiful women of Ur. He had been a grown man, already married to Sarah, when Thare said that they must leave Ur, that they would no longer support themselves by selling lambs and goats to the Chaldeans.

Thare had explained that Yahweh, the god of their tribe, had come to him in a vision and ordered him to move. He said the Yahweh considered foul and evil the ways of the Chaldeans, with their temple prostitutes and their sacrifice of children to bloodthirsty gods. His people, the worshipers of Yahweh, must have no part in such hateful practices. They must not even live near those who did such things lest they be corrupted.

As a loyal son of his father and member of his clan, Abraham had packed his tents, gathered his herds into a tight bunch, and mounted his camel, marching behind his father until they came to the region of Haran. Here, Thare said, they could settle and worship their god in peace.

"I was a little puzzled, my lords," said Abraham, "that Yahweh should be such a jealous god. After all, until that time, we dwelt among our neighbors on a live-and-let-live basis. We sacrificed to our god, and they worshiped theirs. Once in a while, if they were having an especially big feast, he would join them. In those days I always thought, Yahweh has our tribe, other gods have other tribes, why should he care? But I came to see differently in Haran, when Yahweh first gave me the promise I have told you of."

Abraham rubbed his hand over his face, as if trying to drive out the ghosts of the past. "In Haran," he continued, "he spoke to me. 'Leave your country, your family, and your father's house,' he said, 'for the land I will show you.' And that was the first time he promised that I would father a multitude.

"As you know, in the desert, a family is one's strength, and it pained me to leave my father and my kinfolk. But Yahweh's will was clear. Besides, there was a promise of many and great offspring, and I had come to fear that Sarah would never bear children.

"I did as my god told me and wandered to this land of Canaan. El Shaddai has promised to give this land to my descendants, although our tribe now possesses but a small portion of the countryside." He swept his arm in a grand gesture, taking in most of the surrounding hills and valleys. "As you see, it is a beautiful land, rich and fertile, with water and pastures for our flocks and herds. What Yahweh has given in part, I am confident he will give in its entirety, in his own time and in his own way. But, I interrupt my tale . . .

"A famine in Canaan drove us to Egypt, myself and my nephew Lot, our wives and kinsmen, our slaves and our herds. There I did something I have regretted ever since, and I can never look into Sarah's eyes without remembering that I was willing to sacrifice her honor for my life. The ruler of the Egyptians—as you probably know, they call him Pharaoh—received us generously enough. After all, we were rich and powerful even in those years, and he knew our stay was temporary. He must have realized that a brief period of hospitality would acquire some strong allies on his northern frontier, so he extended to us the hand of friendship. Unfortunately, with Sarah, he was interested in more than friendship. She was an exceedingly beautiful woman then, and Pharaoh longed to number her among his wives. Afraid for my own life, I sent her to his palace telling him he could have her, that she was my sister, not my wife.

"Well, Pharaoh's bliss was short-lived," Abraham recalled with a chuckle. "I may have been willing to sacrifice my wife to the ruler of the Egyptians, but Yahweh had other plans. Sarah is destined to be the mother of many nations, and my god wanted her preserved for that role. He inflicted seven plagues on Pharaoh and his household—boils, fevers, sweatings—one worse than the other. I'm afraid the poor chap never knew what hit him. Finally, Sarah realized what was happening and told him who she was.

"Pharaoh sent for me. 'What have you done to me?' he asked. 'Why did you not tell me she was your wife?' Pharaoh was enraged at my deception, but he was also afraid of my god. He simply banished me from Egypt and did us no harm.

"We all came back to Canaan—Lot, myself, and

our families. There we split up. My nephew could not keep his servants in line. They were continually fighting with mine over who owned what water hole. To keep peace, I gave him his pick, the land to the west or the land to the east. Lot choose the east, the Plain of Jordan, where he is right now. I was left with the west, the land of Canaan. Right after that Yahweh spoke to me in a dream and said that north, west, and south as far as the eye could see would one day be mine and that it would belong to my descendants forever. 'I will make your descendants like the dust on the ground,' is how he put it. 'When men succeed in counting the specks of dust on the ground then they will be able to count your descendants.'

"I grew richer and richer as the years passed, my lords, until I owned what you now see: vast flocks of sheep, many fine herds of goats and camels, slaves, and a veritable army of kinsmen. But still no son came to me and Sarah. Finally I could stand it no longer. I reproached God. 'My Lord, Yahweh, what do you intend to give me?' I asked. 'I go childless. You have given me no descendants; some man of my household will be my heir.'

"But God is compassionate and understanding. He came to me in a vision and said, 'Look up to heaven and count the stars if you can. Such will be your descendants.'

"My wife gave me her slave girl, Hagar, that I might father a child with her, for such is permitted by our law, my lords. A son came, but when I asked the Lord if this was not to be the first of my descendants who would outnumber the stars, he said no.

Ishmael, for that is what I named the child, would indeed be the father of great peoples. But the mighty nation I should father would have Sarah as its mother. He even told me to call Sarah's son *Issac*, something I would have been quite willing to do if only she would have had the son."

This time Abraham's laugh was pinched with sadness, expressing a long-standing belief that life was more than a little crazy and unpredictable, no matter how powerful your god or what he promised. A sad expression came over his face, and he looked at his guests.

"So you see, my lords, I sit and wait. The last promise was given nearly a year ago. My herds fatten, my flocks increase beyond counting, and my tribe grows stronger and wealthier with each passing day. Somehow, someday, I suppose the Lord will keep that promise. That, I do not doubt. The sands of time, however, continue to run swiftly, and I confess that I find the whole thing more than a trifle absurd. As for my kinsmen, they think I am quite mad, a doddering old fool who has converted his impossible wish into a vision from Yahweh in which a son is promised. So be it. Let them think me mad. They won't be the first—or the last—to interpret my actions as the fruit of a deranged brain. But I tell you, I have been taking the Lord at his word for a long time now. With each year, it grows harder and harder to keep the faith in his promise."

Abraham's narrative was interrupted when Sarah brought a platter of goat's meat and a steaming tray of fresh bread. Abraham made sure that his visitors were comfortable as he served their food. He stood by the oak while they dined, explaining, "An old man like me needs but little food. Go ahead and eat your fill."

As he leaned against the tree, Abraham had the feeling that his eyes were playing tricks on him. The three figures reclining on the mats seemed to shimmer in the desert haze. He told himself the heat was getting to him. Perhaps he shouldn't have had so much wine. He blinked hard and shook his head, but the result was even more startling. When the old chieftain opened his eyes, the three noble guests had merged into one, a gleaming giant of a man who rose to his feet, towering over his host.

"Abraham," the apparition asked, "where is your wife, Sarah?"

"Why, my lord," the startled chieftain replied, "she's in the tent."

"Next year, without fail, I shall visit you again at this time. Your wife will then have a son."

From inside the tent, Sarah laughed—as her husband had earlier—at the absurdity of the promise.

The tall stranger rebuked her. "Is anything too wonderful for Yahweh?" he asked, making his voice loud enough to be certain Sarah heard the question. Just as loudly, he repeated his promise to return in a year and visit Sarah and her new son. Then, before Abraham could grasp what was happening, the giant of a man became again the three strangers reclining on their soft rugs, finishing the last of the bread and goat's meat. Abraham leaned against the old oak tree, wondering if his eyes and ears had really seen and heard what he thought they had.

This Yahweh was surely a strange god, he told

himself, staring in amazement at the three visitors. Each of the young men wore a smile that hinted at mysterious and wonderful knowledge. Suddenly Abraham realized what the knowledge was. The mysterious visitors who had strolled into his camp that day were one and the same as the handsome being who had promised him a son before the next twelve months were over. He did not know how he realized who they were or why Yahweh had chosen such a peculiar way to repeat his promise. But Abraham, son of Thare, knew that the promise was just as real as the rough bark of the oak that supported his body.

He would be a father. Sarah would be a mother. They would have their child, Isaac, and he would father other sons until one day they would seem as numerous as the stars in the sky or the sands of the desert. All these wonderful things would happen because he, Abraham, had believed; because he had remained true to an absurd promise that had been repeated in many places over many decades because he had not lost faith even when the years had bent his back and whitened his beard.

Isaac would be born—he knew it. That certainty made everything he had endured—leaving Ur, giving up father and kinfolk, wandering to Canaan and to Egypt and back to Canaan, putting up with the mockery of his tribesmen—worthwhile, because Isaac would be born.

Do You Want to Be a Hero?

Heroism can be fun. The wide receiver who makes the shoestring catch and runs thirty-six yards for the game-winning touchdown gets lot of applause, maybe a trophy, and a date with the most popular girl in school. Even a soldier, if he survives, returns to a victory parade and a chest full of medals.

Heroism can be fatal. A New Jersey policeman drowned trying to rescue two small children who were washed into a sewer by a flash flood. He didn't save the tots, and the medal didn't help his wife or his own children very much. He didn't think of that when he saw the terrified youngsters on the frail rubber raft. He jumped into the water because it was his job.

There are no advance guarantees about what kind of approval you'll receive if you make a decision to live your life all out for what you believe in. Only time will tell whether your heroism is the fun kind or the fatal variety. There are a few probabilities, though. Be ready for pain and suffering. Heroism doesn't come easy. It always demands sacrifice. Be ready for unpopularity. The hero doesn't get that way by joining someone else's parade. In the words of Henry David Thoreau, "Some men march to the sound of a different drummer." All heroes do. Be ready for the long haul. You can't guarantee that your heroism will come from one daring act at a moment of crisis. More often than not, heroism is of the day-in-day-out variety. It consists in doing what we believe we ought to be doing as well as we can, one day at a time. It may not produce any trophies. But it will almost guarantee that, if a moment of glory presents itself, you'll be ready. Plant your own field. Martin de Porres did that. He didn't have to be a bishop, a nobleman, or a general. He stayed a lay brother all his life, but he found his own path to heroism.

Centuries ago, a young man named Augustine was led to his brand of heroism by hearing about the lives of others who had dared to do great things. Augustine was walking in the garden behind his house. Over the stone wall between his yard and his neighbor's came the voice of someone reading the lives of the saints. (People used to read aloud in ancient days.) Fascinated, Augustine listened to the stories of how brave young men and women had given their all for God during the Roman persecutions of Christianity. Suddenly, the thought dawned on him: If these young men and women can do it, why can't I? So he did. Augustine went out and became a brave and holy man, one of the most brilliant minds in the history of the Catholic Church.

Maybe one of these ten lives will spark the same question in you: If they could do it, why can't I?